1973

GUIDE TO DRUG REHABILITATION

Guide to Drug Rehabilitation

A Public Health Approach

by Roger E. Meyer, M.D.

Foreword by Jerome H. Jaffe, M.D.

Beacon Press   Boston

Copyright © 1972 by Roger E. Meyer, M.D.

Library of Congress catalog card number: 76–179152

International Standard Book Number: 0–8070–2772–3

Beacon Press books are published under the auspices
of the Unitarian Universalist Association

Published simultaneously in Canada by Saunders of Toronto, Ltd.

All rights reserved

Printed in the United States of America

To my wife Sheila
and my daughters Tobie and Stephanie

Contents

Foreword

BY JEROME H. JAFFE, M.D.

The past decade has seen an explosion of interest in the use of psychoactive substances. While this increase in interest has taken place in virtually every industrialized society in the world, in the United States it has reached a point where the drug abuse problem is now rated by many citizens to be as important as that of war and peace, economic stability, and racial tension.

Along with the increased interest, we have seen a phenomenal rise in the number of articles and books dealing with the topic—leading more than a few cynics to speculate that the public concern is due more to the articles than the growing use of drugs. Under such circumstances, the publication of another book on "the drug problem" would ordinarily elicit little enthusiasm either from the general public or from those scientists and public officials charged with evolving more effective responses to the problem. But these are not ordinary circumstances, and this is not just another book.

The United States is presently struggling to develop a coordinated and integrated response to the fact that the psychoactive substances and the American people coexist and are likely to for many years to come. The need for an effort at coordination stems from the growing awareness that all of the elements making up the national response—treatment of drug users, attempts to control drug availability or commercialization, and official regulation of drug consumption—are always in a state of dynamic equilibrium. Efforts to change just one element may set in motion a train of interreacting processes in which new balances emerge, and unexpected and sometimes unwanted events occur. Although this book deals mainly with the treatment of drug users, it strives to place this one element within the context of an interreacting process.

It is a clinical truism that the less effective our treatment methods for any given syndrome, the wider the diversity of opinion on how best to approach it. So it is with the treatment of compulsive drug use. The American response has been the development of a number of conceptually distinct approaches or models. These models differ not only in the ways in which the individual drug user is handled, but also in the premises upon which treatment operations are based, and even upon the very goals that the treatment systems try to reach. In order to compare these approaches with respect to effectiveness, it is not necessary that they be based on similar ideologies or even that they proceed from identical premises. However, comparison is meaningful only if the various approaches are striving to reach the same goals.

Ideally, every approach would attempt to help all compulsive drug users to become law-abiding, emotionally stable, socially independent, non-drug-using, and productive members of the community. Yet there is disagreement about which of these goals should be given emphasis when all cannot be met. It is becoming apparent that different patterns of outcome for different kinds of patients participating in different programs is the usual situation. It would seem that all that is required is to decide which goals are most important and to arrange for each patient to participate in those programs most likely to yield the best outcome for that patient.

Unfortunately, so logical an approach to the problems of treatment and rehabilitation will be difficult to achieve. Over the years different treatment approaches have been espoused, promoted, and financed by different agencies, both public and private. A number of historical processes have led to the present situation in which the various treatment models have become imbedded in a political-economic matrix in which the inherent attributes of the models are overshadowed by other considerations.

To present the issues in their full complexity in an informed and balanced way requires a wide range of experience, unusual analytic capacities, and the courage to be candid even when candor offends. It is such a range of experience, analytic capacities, courage, and candor that the author brings to this task. Although one need not have a medical background to appreciate this book, it is not a book for the layman. Rather, it is addressed to those persons who are seriously interested in one of the major social and health care issues of our society.

Many will take issue with some of the conclusions the author has drawn from his observations, but few indeed will not find it honest and enlightening.

Washington, D.C.
December 1971

Preface

It is difficult in writing a book on contemporary problems of drug abuse and addiction to aim a message at any single audience. The problem has become so popularized in lay literature that at various times lay persons are more expert than professionals; and each is usually more knowledgeable about some area of special interest within the field while uninformed or misinformed about the rest. Nevertheless, with a rapidly expanding problem of heroin addiction in this country and a continuing problem of hallucinogenic drug abuse (plus an undefined amount of stimulant and sedative misuse and dependency) there is an urgent need to develop new, locally constituted, treatment rehabilitation and prevention facilities.

As this book was being completed, the organizational structures at the Federal level for funding community-based treatment were to be reorganized under a new Special Action Office on Drug Abuse Prevention reporting directly to the White House. At this writing, it is impossible to predict the outcome of this reorganization. The choice of Dr. Jerome Jaffe as the first Director of the office was, however, a recognition that scientific and management expertise is urgently needed to come to grips with the drug abuse epidemic. This appointment was the first in over fifty years committing an administration to a public health approach to the problem rather than a narrow enforcement model. The fumbling for direction in the past five to six years is documented in the final chapter of the book and will hopefully not have to be repeated.

No book can hope to cover all aspects of the drug abuse problem. The kaleidoscopic changes on the drug scene and the seemingly perverse proclivity of man to seek out new ways to produce a "high" promises an unpredictable future. The recent discovery of aerosol inhalation by young teenagers whose older siblings had explored solvent sniffing (including model-airplane glue and gasoline) only confirms the futility of banning Ban spray and other universally available products. Rather, we should concentrate on the selective enforcement of laws dealing with hard drugs. The central issue obviously concerns our need to deal with the compelling psychological and social forces which push some adolescents to this form of "recreation." While describing some approaches to primary prevention, the main body of the book deals with established treatment modalities for the more serious drug dependency syndromes. The most serious problem (alcoholism) is ignored because it has become standard in this era of selective attention to create separate subspecialties in alcoholism and drug addiction. While there may be sociocultural and therapeutic reasons for this, it is well for the reader to keep in mind that this society suffers more from the ravages of the legal intoxicant (alcohol) than from controlled drugs.

This book is aimed at persons who are or will be in a policy-making capacity at the local and regional levels. It is written so as to be useful to physicians, other medical personnel, behavioral scientists, social workers, paraprofessionals, and policy makers who are in a position to launch (or interfere with) the development of locally constituted programs. It is written with the hope that it is not too late to develop a rational public-health-oriented approach which will consider political realities, but will not allow these to destroy or abort the development of an effective service network. The new Federal effort will obviously require the development of new locally constituted treatment facilities. These facilities will require individuals with technical expertise as well as political sophistication.

My own experience at the Federal and local levels has convinced me of the extreme complexity in implementing narcotic addiction treatment programs. Hopefully, some of the problems may be ameliorated by the establishment of Dr. Jaffe's office at the White House. More likely there will continue to be the same range of problems facing local program directors as they seek to do something about the problem of heroin addiction and other drug abuse and dependence. My own thinking has evolved over the last five years and has been influenced by the work of Dr. Jaffe in Illinois, Dr. Gerald Caplan of Harvard, Dr. Herbert Kleber in New Haven, Drs. Vincent Dole and Marie Nyswander of Rockefeller University, and Dr. David Smith's group in San Francisco. At the political level, work with Drs. Daniel Freedman of the University of Chicago and Jonathan Cole of Boston State Hospital and Attorney Neil Chayet has emphasized the importance of a continuing sophisticated lobbying effort at the Federal, State, and local levels. My experiences working with State and Federal governments have made me relatively hopeful that when faced with a crisis, the system can move in response to appropriate pressures. On the other hand, my experiences at the local community level have convinced me of the futility of attempts to placate the irrational rage and political sophistry of *some* community leaders if this leads to compromises in quality care.

Hopefully, persons involved in developing new treatment approaches will appreciate the need for a rational approach based upon the pharmacological realities of the drugs, the sociological realities of subcultures, and the complex psychic interactions, all of which affect the treatment process. It is also hoped that persons who get involved in these programs will also learn and master the political realities which can affect their programs and will seek consultation from knowledgeable persons who have "been over the same route."

The able assistance of Miss Barbara Bacewicz in preparing, editing, and researching for this document has been greatly appreciated. And it would not be possible to spend nights, weekends, and holidays preparing a book without the tolerance and forbearance of a loving family.

GUIDE TO DRUG REHABILITATION

The drug abuse epidemic and the need for a public health approach

The drug problem has managed to capture more lines of newsprint than any other contemporary health problem. Its social ramifications are profound and arouse the concern of all who perceive an unraveling of the fabric of our society. The drug problem is thought to be symptomatic of the chaos afflicting our nation; polemicists of the far right perceive a Communist plot, while liberal and radical authors blame racism, the Vietnam war, and other social ills for the "raging epidemic." The marihuana laws are both challenged and defended with all the force of political argument. Treatment programs are proposed, defended, and challenged in the popular press while real treatment effectiveness is documented in very few places. Professionals are sought as members of panels (along with policemen, politicians, and ex-addicts) but most professionals are either woefully ignorant or passionately polemical about the problem. Anxious communities and school systems readily appropriate funds to learn about drug programs from local or regional panelists, while potentially effective programs are bogged down in unreasonable bureaucratic red tape.

At the Federal level, a number of programs have been funded out of separate agencies with different funding requirements and different treatment orientation. On the one hand the National Institute of Mental Health, at the instigation of Congress, supports a national civil commitment program based at the Lexington and Fort Worth Hospitals while at the same time supporting a progressive matching fund program for staffing community-based drug treatment at locally constituted mental health centers. The Office of Economic Opportunity, from a different perspective, provides up to fourteen months of support for the development of drug treatment programs in neighborhood health centers. These centers were previously developed for general health services under the auspices of OEO. Drug, treatment programs are also being sponsored within the Federal Bureau of Prisons and more recently by the Veterans Administration. Other Federal funds have recently become available through the Department of Housing and Urban Development and separately through the Department of Justice via the Safe Streets Act.

At the State level, legislatures have been reluctant to commit significant sums for rehabilitation of the addict. Local politicians sometimes play upon the fears of the electorate and ignore the complexity of the problem. Old-line bureaucrats in State agencies unaccustomed to funding ex-addict therapists and street workers block program development and the spending of already appropriated funds. At the community level, lower and middle class groups oppose housing therapeutic communities run by ex-addicts in their midst while some minority group leaders fight the introduction of methadone maintenance treatment programs on the grounds that these are "attempts by the white establishment to enslave young blacks."

The scene is reminiscent of a slapstick comedy in which a theater full of screaming, bickering people is burning to the ground because the fire engines are out of gasoline, or are otherwise prevented from coming to the rescue. Over the past five to ten years a number of rather specific treatment modalities have been developed for heroin addiction, and several types of ad hoc services have appeared for treating the complications of hallucinogenic drug abuse. In a few cities, truly model programs have been developed with Federal and State money. These programs have incorporated the newer treatment technologies and applied them to local conditions. Yet, despite these very real advances, most localities continue to grope along with inadequate information. Legislators, mayors, governors, professionals, and lay persons are all too readily impressed with programs that "promise to get the addict off the streets" or offer "youth-run projects where kids can help kids unencumbered by adults."

The irony in this age of accelerated communication is that there has been virtually no communication which offers some rational orientation based upon the hard data generated by the reasonably effective programs. Despite the availability of some Federal and State funds, many communities end up denying the existence of a drug problem until faced with a "bust" or "O.D." (drug overdosage) at the local high school. At that point committees are formed by concerned parents, and inquiries are made regarding cause, cost, and solution. Unfortunately, it is the rare community that evolves an approach to the drug problem or even a part of it. The committee generates some enthusiasm at the outset but it is usually not sustained long enough. In the end citizens deplore the "parents who don't keep track of their children" and the community returns to its former calm where drugs were "somebody else's problem."

How did the drug abuse problem become a national obsession during the late 1960's? What caused this epidemic to break out of the circumscribed areas of endemic drug usage in the blighted urban ghettoes of our country? Was there some common tainted well from which so many of our young people drank and became afflicted? Explanations abound, but real understanding which might lead to prevention is clearly lacking. The explanations are in fact only observations which note associations between drug abuse and patterns of social, familial, or individual behavior. Clearly, drug availability, society, and individual personality are all involved to a degree. When a substance is used by a large percentage of the population (e.g., alcohol), the question of usage per se is not associated with individual psychopathology. Thus, since marihuana has been used by upward of 40 to 50 percent of persons in their twenties, mere use by persons in this age group is not indicative of a need for psychiatric help. Heavy use of alcohol or marihuana is probably associated with some emotional distress. Additionally, where a substance is used by a small percentage of the population (e.g., heroin, hallucinogens, etc.), there is a greater likelihood that use per se is indicative of a deeper psychiatric disturbance. As a corollary to this, it may be that whites who use heroin are generally more psychiatrically disabled before getting into the drug than urban blacks, since heroin has been more readily available in the ghetto than in largely white areas and heroin experimentation may be more commonly a part of ghetto life.[1]

The importance of supply in the genesis of the addictions is noted in the observation that the peak prevalence of opiate addiction in the United States probably occurred prior to World War I. The availability of opiates in various patent medicines and widespread uncontrolled prescription of opiate pain killers by physicians were the principal factors behind this historical epidemic. With the passage of the Harrison Narcotics Act, enforcement was reasonably effective in controlling the epidemic and eventually reversing it. With the introduction of law enforcement as the principal vehicle of control, however, organized medicine abdicated any formal role in the treatment of the addictions (with two notable exceptions) until the 1960's. In the 1920's the American Medical Association supported the establishment of drug addiction treatment clinics manned by physicians. The effectiveness of these clinics is still controversial but they were ultimately closed by enforcement authorities allegedly because they were leading to further dissemination of drugs. A very different approach was begun by the Federal government in the mid-thirties with the construction of two hospitals in Lexington, Kentucky, and Fort Worth, Texas. These large, prison-like institutions served to keep patients far from their homes and the spawning ground of their addiction in an environment where patients might be detoxified, rehabilitated, and then returned to their homes. Unfortunately, the vast majority of patients returned to drugs when back in their home communities.

The role of law enforcement in controlling drug usage in this country has often been criticized. A number of sociologists have argued that the association between crime and heroin addiction derives directly from laws which make possession of the drug a crime while controlling the supplies to the point where the cost of a habit may run as high as $100 a day. They

[1] See *Manchild in the Promised Land* by Claude Brown.

have argued that legalized heroin prescription would eliminate the criminal behavior. The hypothesis, however, is unproven. Many heroin addicts were delinquents before they were addicts. Moreover, the British experience with heroin prescription resulted in a fivefold increase in the problem (including a criminal problem) through the early 1960's. This small-scale epidemic caused the British to limit heroin prescription to a few specific clinics rather than many centers and general practitioners as before. Still, with only 2,800 known addicts in Britain, there is a greater likelihood of limiting the problem than in this country. The British are increasingly using methadone substitution in the treatment of heroin users.

Law enforcement in the United States has also been criticized for focusing attention on marihuana users rather than going after major international traffickers in heroin. This type of argument is difficult to prove. It is clear, however, that law enforcement has a major role to play in controlling supplies of legal and illegal drugs. This should involve restrictions on the growth of the opium poppy to meet the legitimate medical need for opiates.[2] Law enforcement also should be involved in restricting and controlling the manufacture and wholesale distribution of amphetamines and barbiturates. Enough of these drugs are manufactured in the United States each year to supply every man, woman, and child in this country with thirty therapeutic doses. Obviously much is being diverted from manufacturers' stocks into the black market. Yet, when Congress was considering new drug abuse legislation in 1969 and 1970, the Pharmaceutical Manufacturers Association successfully lobbied against greater restrictions in this area and the Department of Justice sought to place greater controls on research and medical practice rather than on manufacturers and wholesalers. This was not really consistent with what should have been the major concern

[2] This could involve agricultural subsidies to Turkish farmers for *not* growing the poppy much as American farmers have been subsidized for not planting certain crops. This approach would take account of some of the economic issues in mountainous regions of Turkey that lead to the illegal growth of the opium poppy.

of law enforcement: diversion of manufacturers' stocks to the black market.

The availability of drugs through illicit trade is clearly one important factor sustaining the present epidemic. It is clear that law enforcement has a preëminent role in this area but it is not clear that law enforcement officials in the United States have so defined their task as to be most effective. When supplies of street heroin are low because of effective law enforcement, the cost of a habit goes up—and so does the crime rate. When heroin is more readily available on the street due to ineffective law enforcement, there is a greater likelihood of a spreading drug epidemic. When supplies of one drug are effectively limited, addicts often drift into other drugs. The situation is obviously complex. However, in case some well-meaning but naive person assumes that law enforcement has a role because Americans have a "peculiarly hysterical" response to drugs, one should be aware that the Japanese in the 1950's and the Swedes in the late 1960's remedied the problem of amphetamine usage by cracking down hard on illegal possession, manufacture, and sale. Moreover, the Chinese in the early 19th century fought a war against British colonialism to restrict the importing and sale of opium which had been encouraged by the British. The tendency in this country to lump permissiveness toward drug use with other leftist causes is inappropriate and politicizes an issue which should be considered in public health terms. The role of law enforcement should always be to work in collaboration with medical authorities while strictly adhering to its role in restricting illicit distribution of all drugs.   ✷

The second consideration (after drug availability) important in understanding the present epidemic is the social factors associated with drug abuse. Of great interest is the observation that the best predictor of the use of any drug of abuse by an individual is the drug use history of his close friends. This may be no more intuitive than the old proverb "birds of a feather flock together," but it is the best social predictor currently available (even though there are obviously exceptions to this rule). More complex analyses of marihuana usage (but not heavy use) among college students in the mid-1960's found it especially high among those majoring in the behavioral sciences and humanities and those with radical political views. Religious persons were found less likely to be marihuana users. These observations sparked a whole range of hypotheses about the reasons for marihuana usage ranging from "a substitute for lost religious feeling," to "alienation" from the political system, and a "search for aesthetic awareness." Carried by the mass media, these "explanations" failed to differentiate between marihuana and other drug use or even between marihuana experimentation and heavy, daily usage. There is obviously a contagion factor affecting individual behavior in a group which is separate from motivation in the individual based upon internal need. And as Frances Cheek and Richard Blum have observed, groups of marihuana (and LSD) users develop a common rationale and set within the group for the drug experience. It is the pattern of association rather than the rationale which accounts for marihuana usage. With the spread of cannabis usage beyond the campus, it is clear that the old hypotheses don't hold up, just as they could not account for marihuana use in the ghetto.

Another social determinant of drug usage which has been developed to account for the current epidemic is the American attitude toward psychic pain and a search for relief through medication. "Better things for better living through chemistry" has been called an American pastime. Thus, drug-using children were found to come from families where one or both parents abused alcohol or tranquilizers. The generation gap was defined as merely a difference in tastes, so far as intoxicants are concerned. In point of fact, drug or alcohol excess in the parents may suggest some degree of psychopathology in the family. In this situation, it is not unreasonable to suppose that the children of disturbed parents may be themselves emotionally disturbed and (in the present epidemic) may not only experiment with marihuana but may get into heavy use of cannabis or other drugs. In other words, in a psychiatric epidemic, those who are already emotionally disturbed will likely be involved and the characteristic behaviors will be found especially in this group.

This is a corollary of the observation that the overt manifestations of emotional disorder are largely culturally determined.[3]

Apart from an association with psychopathology, it is difficult to attribute the current epidemic to some American penchant for psychic pain relief. There is no evidence that the adult population of the United States is more tranquilized than that of any other country. And the current drug abuse problem is present in Western Europe, thereby negating social explanations that stop at the western shores of the Atlantic Ocean.

Finally, there are social explanations which take account of differences in drug usage patterns between cultures and in different cultures at different times in their history. Cannabis use was not indigenous to Western Africa. Yet with the development of large urban areas with high rates of unemployment among persons recently migrating from rural areas, one now finds cannabis use and abuse. In Japan, after World War II, there was much social and cultural disorganization stemming from defeat (the defeat of the Emperor—God) and the American occupation. In this setting the large quantities of amphetamine (previously stored by the Japanese army for its soldiers) had a ready market among the young. Germany in the 1920's also had its experiences with drug abuse. Chein *et al.*, in this country, found heroin usage highest in those poor communities with the greatest degree of familial disorganization, crime, welfare, and despair among the young. Poverty per se was not the significant variable, but poverty associated with cultural disorganization was significantly correlated with heroin addiction. In conditions such as these, it is the adolescent who is somehow vulnerable to drug abuse: alcoholism among young American Indians; heroin usage among young blacks, Puerto Ricans, Mexican Americans; and the emergence of methamphetamine and heroin abuse among those who were formerly called Hippies. In other words, intoxication appears to be the response of adolescents who feel that the culture transmitted to them has no value. Adolescence is a time for questioning; but it is also a time for

---

[3] For example, schizophrenia may be world-wide in distribution but the pattern of symptoms and thought content are peculiar to each society.

affirming membership in a cultural group. Where the norms, values, or physical attributes of the cultural group (or subgroup) are felt to have no value, one can find historical examples of epidemics of intoxication among the young. Without being more specific in terms of the present epidemic, one is obviously tempted to wonder about our present predicament in the United States and Western Europe.

Finally, in any consideration of social determinants of drug abuse one must ask "why some and not others?" This is a question usually avoided in the joys of generalization and has not been studied sufficiently well in the present epidemic or in the past. One of the rare exceptions was a study by Robbins and Murphy who interviewed a group of blacks who had grown up in a St. Louis ghetto twenty-five years earlier and inquired into their drug-using pattern over the quarter century since grade school. Over 50 percent had used marihuana and 20 percent of these had used heroin. The authors found a high correlation between dropping out of high school and heroin usage. Those who did not get to high school and those who graduated high school were relatively immune in that population. It is impossible to draw any conclusions from this study which would shed light on the present epidemic. Obviously research is needed so that society may identify the vulnerable groups and individuals and tailor prevention programs to them.

Studies of individual addicts, unfortunately, also fail to shed light on factors which differentiate users from nonusers of drugs. In research on heroin addicts admitted to the Lexington Hospital, psychopathic deviancy scores on the MMPI[4] were found to be high. Early psychoanalytic writers felt that drugs were a "defense against sadistic impulses and psychosis" while more recent writers ascribe specific drug-seeking to specific states of fixation or regression where the drug effect in the individual meets a psychic need of an earlier stage in childhood.[5]

[4] Essentially a measure of antisocial behavioral tendencies as measured by the Minnesota Multiphasic Personality Inventory.

[5] For example, Frosch argues that patients who have difficulty with individuation and fear of separation may prefer hallucinogenic drugs because of the sense of fusion experienced in the intoxicated state associated with these drugs.

Any of these factors by itself fails to predict drug abuse in a population or an individual. Of greater interest would be longitudinal studies of pre-teenagers through adolescence in order to determine what factors in the group and the individual predispose to drug abuse. These studies have not been carried out.

In general, there is considerable knowledge regarding the medical and social consequences of heroin and other opiate addiction, as well as barbiturate and sedative dependency and alcoholism. Research and clinical information is being collated on the hazards of amphetamine abuse and hallucinogen usage and the marihuana problem is being redefined wherein casual use and experimentation appear to pose minimal medical or psychiatric risk in a young adult population. Later chapters will consider some elementary pharmacology, as well as medical consequences and treatment approaches to the various drug dependencies. Much more is known in these areas than in the area of etiology. Yet public health approaches to the treatment and prevention of many conditions in medicine have developed without a complete understanding of the causes of the disorder, the factors which differentiate risk among individuals and populations, or even the development of a cure for the disorder. The public health approach is practical in that it identifies a problem and develops a solution appropriate to the level of the problem. The alternatives would be total reliance upon law enforcement authorities wherein the problem is defined as criminal; the designation of the problem as strictly medical, involving the physician in a traditional medical relationship; or defining the problem as strictly within the purview of some educational, religious, or other circumscribed professional group whose narrow approach is severely limiting in dealing with the problem on many levels. The public health approach is global and seeks to identify the potential contributions from multiple areas in the society ultimately leading to the prevention and control of the disorder. Obviously the public health approach must be tailored to the needs of specific communities. A prevention program in a minority group ghetto must emphasize the hazards of heroin, while in a suburban community it may focus on a wide variety of drugs (including alcohol excess). Films valuable in prevention programs in one community obviously would be inappropriate in other communities. Law enforcement controlling the supply of drugs coming into a community has a major role to play in a public health approach.

A public health approach identifies three levels of prevention: primary, secondary, and tertiary. Primary prevention means the prevention of inappropriate drug use and drug abuse in vulnerable populations. Secondary prevention seeks to stop drug abuse in an individual before he has become addicted or become identified with a drug-abusing and addicted subculture. Tertiary prevention aims to treat individuals who are addicted to drugs (or involved heavily in subcultures of drug abuse) in such a way as to control the disability and facilitate psychological and social rehabilitation. In this latter group, one must presume that there will likely be some residual deficits and one attempts to limit the degree of disability and the likelihood of relapse. In this circumstance, however, relapse may likely occur but should be considered in the same way as relapse in any chronic medical illness for which there is no cure. As with conditions such as rheumatoid arthritis, for example, some patients' disorders may be arrested and some individuals may have infrequent relapses following treatment. Animal models of the addictions confirm the likelihood of relapse to drug addiction and should be indicative of the hazards of relapse in man. The moral issue somehow intrudes in this condition where it does not in other medical illnesses.

Most treatment programs aimed at chronic drug users really involve tertiary prevention. Secondary prevention at this point in our knowledge is hypothetical since many patients do not come to medical attention between the time that they are experimenting with drugs and the time that they get immersed in an addiction or a subculture of drug abuse. Any description of the drug abuse epidemic must differentiate drugs and extent of use. Marihuana experimentation or casual (weekend) usage by persons in their twenties may not constitute a public health problem, even though such widespread violation of the law has obvious implications for society. Heroin experimentation involves a great risk of eventual addiction and hallucinogen usage by the young or the psychologically vulnerable may result in intractable emotional disorder. Secondary prevention and tertiary prevention should aim to limit progression to more dangerous drugs by those who are involved to a limited degree in drug experimentation. As an aside, it should be noted that marihuana experimentation or casual usage does not lead to heavy or more dangerous drug usage but that heavy, daily marihuana use is often associated with other forms of drug experimentation.

Primary prevention of drug abuse and addiction has received great emphasis in the press and in recent Congressional legislation which will help to fund a national drug education program.[6] Primary prevention has also received a good bit of attention from entrepreneurs interested in selling books, films, and other teaching devices to school systems. In communities where drug addiction or drug abuse has been identified as a problem, teachers, principals, and school committees invest in the relatively small cost of a drug addiction education package to avoid being scapegoated by the community. Many of these packages are untested and unproven in any population of young people. This is not to discourage attempts at drug abuse prevention through education. It is rather to emphasize the complexity of the problem and the danger of relying solely on prepackaged programs. No one, at this time, has a solution.

Any program of primary prevention must aim at the vulnerable adolescent. With drug experimentation now occurring in some communities at the junior high school level, most people agree that education must begin sometime in the elementary grades and progress through high school. Films and other educational materials are very likely to impress children who are not likely to get into the drugs. Children who are likely to get into drugs will be uninfluenced by these teaching materials, while children who are teetering on the brink of drug experi-

---

[6] There was recently a proposal from a group in New York City to "immunize" children with long-acting narcotic-blocking drugs (see Chapter 2) which would prevent youngsters living in areas of high prevalence of heroin addiction from feeling the effects of injected heroin. This rather narrow pharmacological view of the problem has not been systematically studied.

mentation may either be discouraged from, or stimulated toward drug experimentation as a result of exposure to drug education programs. The role of ex-addicts as teachers or lecturers in drug abuse prevention programs is somewhat controversial. Many white middle class adults enthusiastically welcome black ex-addicts to lecture at suburban schools while many blacks fear that ex-addicts will only serve to further glamorize drugs to ghetto youth. It is felt that a black man who has been a junkie and lived to tell about it encourages vulnerable young blacks to try it themselves. In fact there are no data which indicate the relative risk or value of the ex-addict as a teacher about drugs. Suffice it to say, he is not a universally accepted drug abuse prevention agent and blacks may have justifiable fears about the ex-addict as a role model. Some white parents may unconsciously see advantages in encouraging their children's association of the black ex-addict as an unacceptable role model.

All too often planning a drug abuse prevention program is done without consulting the intended audience. Films, pamphlets, speakers, and other educational approaches should be screened by selected members of the student population to help determine the general acceptability and usefulness of such materials. All information distributed to students must take into account the kind and level of knowledge and experience of the group. For example, scare tactics with regard to marihuana usually lead to skepticism about any information presented since most students know people who have tried marihuana, or have used it themselves. The drug experience should be presented accurately so that the dangers of drug abuse are learned and the motivations of the drug user are more readily understood. Students may than reject the suggestions of their peers that they turn on while not rejecting their peers.

In summary, the minimum requirement for a drug abuse program involves the dissemination of accurate information about drug and alcohol use and abuse in a manner which has been developed in conjunction with members of the student audience. Students should screen the available materials along with faculty and administration. The Federal government, through the National Institute of Mental Health, makes available information and film reviews which may be helpful in planning educational programs. Several State education departments have also developed educational packages which might be useful.

In addition to providing information about drugs, communities should attempt to provide concrete alternatives to drug experimentation. Recreational facilities may be useful, but programs in community service involving young people can usually tap a wellspring of idealism while discouraging drug usage. The observation was often made during the campaign of Senator Eugene McCarthy for the Democratic nomination for the Presidency in 1968 that young college students were turning away from drugs in order to be more effective campaigners. Observations about "bad trips" among their friends, fears of genetic hazard, and a wish to "keep clean for Gene" were the reasons most often cited for the decline in the popularity of hallucinogenic drugs during the spring and summer of 1968 after a rapid escalation in hallucinogenic drug use during the previous two years.

Positive alternatives to the life style associated with drug abuse also make for a more effective program in primary prevention than reliance on information on realistic hazards alone. Yet even with this more powerful package young people who are doing badly in school or are in danger of dropping out may be prime candidates for drug experimentation. Where parents, teachers, clergy, and others in contact with these young people have determined that there is an underlying problem, referral to a mental health facility may be indicated. In this regard, mental health consultation to schools, clergy, and other groups may be important in identifying individuals who may be particularly vulnerable to drug experimentation and particularly resistant to educational efforts and other attempts at primary prevention. Special efforts may then be directed to get at the underlying problem before it is complicated by drug experimentation and abuse.

Thus a complete program of primary prevention in a community should include not only the dissemination of accurate information to the young but also should provide realistic alternatives to drug experimentation, while identifying vulnerable school children for special attention. Another aspect of primary prevention has to do with educating physicians in prescribing tranquilizing and stimulant medication to adults and children. Drugs are no substitute for other forms of adaptation and may be anti-therapeutic at times. Physicians often feel pressured into "giving the patient something" because of the patient's insistent demands. Physicians should explore with the patient issues in the current life situation that may underlie psychic distress. Often, the problem is better handled without medication but where medication is indicated, open-ended prescriptions are contraindicated and at times invite drug abuse. Where parents use drugs inappropriately for chronic relief of psychic pain, children may be more vulnerable to drug abuse on the street. Many adolescent drug abusers report the first drug they used was obtained from a parent's prescription of sleeping pills, diet pills, or tranquilizers.

In summary, the drug abuse epidemic in the United States in the past five years has challenged communities, politicians, and service organizations to develop constructive approaches to the problem. For the most part, hysteria has prevailed and reason has floundered. The problem is extremely complex and a solution involves the mobilization of law enforcement resources, medical resources, educational resources, and other constructive forces within the community to limit the spread of the epidemic and to treat the afflicted. A public health approach is clearly in order, including all levels of public health intervention. The next few chapters will provide an overall description of the known types of rehabilitation or tertiary prevention services that have been found useful in treating the complications of drug dependence.

PART ONE

Treating heroin addiction

CHAPTER ONE

Rehabilitating the heroin addict: an overview

The rehabilitation services for heroin addiction are concerned with treating various conditions which may result from or are associated with chronic self-administration of heroin. They may involve any or all of the following four general kinds of services: (1) the treatment of overdosage; (2) the treatment of the withdrawal syndrome; (3) the treatment of medical complications associated with unsterile injections and/or poor living conditions; and (4) the modification of chronic relapsing behaviors of drug use and crime (usually stealing or fraud).[1] In assessing the existing services and future service requirements for the heroin addict in your community you should consider the degree to which these kinds of service are available. The reader should understand that the overall purpose of these four kinds of service is the limitation of disability associated with heroin addiction. None of the services should be considered or evaluated as a cure resulting in a psychiatrically normal patient. Each service must be measured on the basis of its effectiveness in reducing the death rate or in controlling the disability associated with heroin addiction. In New York City, heroin addiction is the leading cause of death in young men between the ages of fifteen and thirty-five. In New York, Massachusetts, and other states, there has been an alarming increase in deaths due to

---

[1] Broadly speaking, the issues here also apply to other forms of opiate dependence. Heroin addiction has a special history of its own, however, and will be the focus of this discussion.

heroin overdosage consistent with the increased incidence of heroin usage. This death rate also suggests the difficulty of bringing the patient to emergency care before it is too late.

THE TREATMENT OF OVERDOSAGE

There would be no problem with overdosage if all heroin were administered in known therapeutic doses by physicians.[2] Since this ideal situation does not exist, we are dealing with a problem in which the dose of heroin administered by the addict is unknown to him and may vary from purchase to purchase depending on the many factors influencing quality control in the underworld market.[3] Accidental overdosage is also associated with the addict's prior experience. An addict who has recently been withdrawn from heroin will likely overdose should he take his regular heroin injection because he is no longer tolerant to his usual "fix." A naive user first experimenting with heroin by injection will have greater difficulty in titrating his dose and runs a greater risk of overdose. Finally, it should be noted that some addicts may intentionally take an excessive heroin injection in an attempt at suicide. When, for whatever reason, an addict has taken an excessive amount of heroin and passes into coma, he runs a risk of death due to respiratory arrest. The treatment of opiate overdosage is actually fairly straightforward. The patient needs to be hospitalized and his behavior monitored over a period of twenty-four to seventy-two hours. For the period of acute intoxication he needs to receive injections of narcotic drug antagonists (such as nalorphine) which rapidly counter the effects of the heroin. The injections of narcotic antagonist need to be repeated when the patient appears to be drifting back into coma. In general, once the patient has

[2] Even in Great Britain where heroin was legal by prescription, a certain amount of the drug became available on the black market resulting in a spreading drug epidemic where some addicts were administering unknown doses (and not, obviously, under medical supervision).

[3] The effectiveness of law enforcement, the laws of supply and demand, and the profit motives of the distributors all influence the street price of heroin.

come to medical attention there is no reason why he should die of overdosage because the treatments available should be totally effective.

There is some controversy within medicine as to whether death from "overdosage" is strictly related to heroin. Some pathologists believe that substances used to dilute heroin (e.g., quinine) may cause abnormalities of heart beat which may result in death. Quinine overdose, of course, does not respond to narcotic antagonists and requires a different form of medical intervention. Where the problem is heroin overdosage, the main problem is getting the patient to emergency medical attention. This is not an easy task since heroin self-administration is often a solitary experience. This creates an impossible situation from a public health standpoint. All that you can reasonably do is to educate physicians about the signs and symptoms of heroin overdose (including depressed respirations and pinpoint pupils) and about certain principles of using narcotic antagonist drugs. Additionally, urban hospitals should not be allowed to exclude heroin addicts from inpatient care. The time may come when heroin addicts are encouraged to carry small packets of naloxone[4] the way diabetics on insulin carry sugar cubes. The naloxone could then be administered in an emergency by a family member or friend pending the arrival of medical assistance.

THE TREATMENT OF WITHDRAWAL STATES

For many years it has been felt that the treatment of heroin withdrawal symptoms should occur in a hospital. The techniques of treatment were developed successfully at the Public Health Service hospitals at Lexington, Kentucky, and Fort Worth, Texas, and involve starting the addict on a dose of methadone consistent with his own heroin habit (usually 20 mg. methadone twice daily or 40 mg. once a day) and reducing the methadone dose by 20 percent per day. There is invariably some complaint of symptomatology, generally mimicking the course of a mild bout of influenza. Despite the development

[4] A narcotic antagonist with no properties of an opiate drug.

of techniques for avoiding "cold turkey" many addicts have had to experience withdrawal symptoms in prisons; while some therapeutic communities (e.g., Synanon and Daytop Village) utilize the "cold turkey" syndrome to encourage the patient to relate to people for relief rather than to drugs. As such, the latter has become a part of the treatment technique in these organizations. Apart from the application of "cold turkey" as a treatment technique in such self-help therapeutic environments, there seems no reason not to relieve the symptoms of withdrawal in the addict, preferably in the context of a broadly based rehabilitation program. With the increasing use of heroin, however, there is a shortage of local hospital beds for inpatient treatment of the withdrawal syndrome. Recent experiences in Chicago, New York, Philadelphia, Boston, and other cities suggest that outpatient detoxification is feasible and less costly and runs no greater risk of relapse to addiction.[5]

Detoxification of heroin addicts on an outpatient basis may be complicated and requires stringent controls in order to avoid potential abuses of the treatment system. Addicts make unreliable patients and there is a ready market for methadone on the street which may lead to secondary methadone epidemics. In fact, in some cities there is an active black market for methadone, where the street price may exceed the pharmacy price by as much as 500 percent. Some methadone preparations may be converted for intravenous administration with an associated "high." The possibility of methadone epidemics has, of course, initiated activity by the Bureau of Narcotics and Dangerous Drugs. Unfortunately, poorly controlled programs have created negative publicity for all outpatient methadone detoxification programs (and, by association, for methadone maintenance treatment programs). At this writing, neither State nor Federal law enforcement or public health agencies have set down strict guidelines to carefully restrict the prescription of methadone in detoxification programs to prevent diversion to

---

[5] Inpatient treatment of withdrawal rarely leads to successful recovery without relapse to addiction. The Public Health Service hospitals boast a 5 percent success rate. Outpatient detoxification does at least as well.

the black market. In one state, the pharmacists' association acted unilaterally to prevent the dispensation of methadone by individual pharmacists because of the problems of outpatient detoxification via prescription. This created an emergency situation where private physicians were no longer able to detoxify patients and there was a shortage of treatment services for outpatient (or inpatient) detoxification.

The absence of Federal or local guidelines on outpatient detoxification with methadone has led to confusion at the local level. In communities where there has been no centralized planning of public health services for heroin addicts, there are methadone epidemics resulting from widespread prescription by general hospitals and private physicians. As a result of a leadership vacuum at several levels of government, all treatment programs have become tarnished by the actions of some poorly controlled detoxification programs. This is not unlike the situation that faced the addiction clinics of the 1920's and which eventually led to their abandonment. The failure to develop guidelines at this late date is inexcusable. It is further evidence of a lack of clear-cut responsibility by a particular Federal or State agency and only serves to discredit medical intervention programs. As such it supports the stereotypes of the old Federal Bureau of Narcotics that drug addiction is merely a law enforcement problem. Outpatient detoxification of the heroin addict must continue. The failure of Federal and State governments to differentiate "good" from "bad" programs could lead to the abandonment of this effort.

Methadone administration for outpatient detoxification should be restricted to specified treatment centers in each city. The number and location of such centers will depend on the prevalence and distribution of the addiction problem in the city. Wherever possible, methadone should only be dispensed at the clinic in the presence of a nurse and the clinic should be open every day of the week.[6] Where this is not possible, the clinic

[6] This procedure applies as well to methadone maintenance treatment described in the next chapter. It is especially true in detoxification programs dealing with patients who, by virtue of the short-term nature of the treatment, cannot be trusted.

should be open for five and a half days and the patient permitted to take home one dose of methadone. In general, methadone may be given once a day, requiring one visit per day by the patient. Patients may be given a supplementary, non-addicting tranquilizer[7] which can be taken while the patient is not at the clinic.

In addition to requiring daily outpatient visits, clinics should monitor the urine of all addict patients in order to document "cheating" with heroin or other drugs of abuse. Urine can be collected daily or twice weekly on a random collection schedule. Most cities now have or have ready access to laboratories skilled in thin layer or gas-liquid chromatography. Urinary screening and daily outpatient visits provide the kind of control and information essential to outpatient detoxification.

The normal course of outpatient detoxification may run from three to twenty-one days,[8] depending upon the initial size of the patient's habit. Almost all clinics report problems holding patients in treatment during this phase, and there has been some experimentation with what has been called long-term detoxification. This technique maintains patients on low doses of methadone (e.g., 30 mg./day) for prolonged periods of time. The dose of methadone is only reduced after the patient's life situation has become stabilized and he is more involved in a therapeutic program. This type of treatment has been defined as detoxification by clinics in Philadelphia and British Columbia but is more correctly called low-dose methadone maintenance in other cities. It will be described later under the section on treatments for chronic relapsing behavior.

Detoxification per se is a straightforward medical treatment. It is often used by addicts as a means of simply reducing the cost of their habit[9] which tends to demoralize treatment personnel working in detoxification facilities who are hoping for

---

[7] Chloropromazine and Promethazine have been prescribed in this way.

[8] Inpatient detoxification should be completed in 3–7 days, but there may be some advantage to a more gradual reduction in methadone dosage in outpatients.

[9] Once a heroin addict has been detoxified he can achieve a "high" with lower and less costly doses of injected heroin.

an "occasional cure." This is unfortunate. Detoxification is not a "cure": it is the medical treatment for opiate withdrawal. The programs at the Lexington and Fort Worth hospitals were extremely effective in the treatment of withdrawal. Their failure rate was in the treatment of chronic relapsing behaviors, wherein 95 percent of patients released from these institutions relapsed to drug use on the street. As detoxification facilities, however, far from the centers of endemic heroin usage, they were unnecessarily costly and inappropriate.

Detoxification services can be more easily and cheaply set up at the community level. Outpatient detoxification is by far the least expensive form of this treatment and is at least as effective as inpatient detoxification in preventing relapse to heroin addiction. In fact, several cities have eliminated inpatient detoxification facilities for uncomplicated heroin withdrawal. For the local community developing detoxification services it is suggested that several beds be available in a local hospital for patients with medically complicated or mixed opiate-sedative drug dependence.[10] Outpatient detoxification should be the treatment of choice for most cases of heroin (or other opiate) withdrawal. One final word seems in order. In a number of cities halfway houses run by ex-addicts have been established using volunteer physicians to provide medical treatment and detoxification. All too frequently the physicians have been young and idealistic but naive in dealing with addicts (or ex-addicts). They have been seduced into prescribing methadone to halfway house residents often in sufficient quantities to maintain a reservoir of methadone on the premises. In this situation, nonphysicians (usually ex-addicts) have been illegally dispensing methadone under a medical cover. This is disastrous! It is highly desirable that self-help groups and halfway houses run by ex-addicts be affiliated with established medical facilities for detoxification. The volunteer young physician becomes trapped and scared by the demands of the ex-addicts. His efforts also undercut any relationship between the self-help group and a well-run clinic in which medical responsibility would appropri-

[10] The treatment of sedative withdrawal is discussed in Chapter 5.   64431

ately be preserved. Needless to say, methadone in halfway houses inevitably leads to abuses and an increase in the quantity of methadone on the street. In this situation, the community is the loser. Where such halfway houses are affiliated with established medical facilities and methadone is dispensed in the clinic, the clinic may be better able to "hold" patients through the course of detoxification while assuring that the patient is involved in a more complete program of social rehabilitation through the halfway house.

SIX GENERAL PRINCIPLES IN THE TREATMENT OF CHRONIC RELAPSING BEHAVIOR

Before considering the specific approaches for the treatment of chronic relapsing behaviors, it is important to consider several general principles. The first of these principles is that heroin addiction is associated with a number of medical conditions stemming from unsterile techniques of self-injection and impoverished living conditions.[11] Thus, whether a program emphasizes civil commitment in a large institution, a voluntary therapeutic community operated by a self-help group, or one of a number of drug maintenance programs operated by a medical facility, it is important that the patient be evaluated medically and that the medical complications of his disorder be treated. This is not only good medical practice but also may facilitate social rehabilitation and the development of a psychiatrically therapeutic relationship.

The second principle relates to psychological and social disabilities requiring a broad range of rehabilitation services for patients motivated to use them. Heroin addicts from lower class

---

[11] The most common medical complications are serum hepatitis and subacute bacterial endocarditis but addicts may present any of a variety of unusual infections or chronic medical disabilities. Venereal disease is also very common in this group where syphilis may be transmitted by using needles previously used by an infected person or in the usual manner by sexual contact with an infected person.

black and Spanish-speaking groups often have a history of delinquency which antedates their addiction and a history of addiction which may have started in the mid-teens. Very often these patients have not completed high school and have spent many years in penal institutions. Whatever family life there is, is usually in shambles. Work history is spotty, usually as unskilled employment during brief periods. Heroin usage is endemic in the inner city and the patient may not have experimented with many types of drugs before arriving at heroin. This contrasts somewhat with the more recent picture emerging in white and black middle class communities. In this situation heroin self-administration begins after progression through hallucinogenic drugs, amphetamines, and barbiturates. These adolescents are psychologically disturbed and usually require some form of psychological intervention. Additionally, many are untrained vocationally and may require some degree of vocational or educational rehabilitation, although they are from more prosperous backgrounds. The psychological treatment will usually involve encounter group techniques, although in some patients, more traditional forms of psychotherapy may be indicated. Many of these patients may present refractory psychiatric complications of hallucinogenic, amphetamine, or barbiturate abuse,[12] although heroin addiction is the manifest and current presenting illness.

In general, the heroin addict presents a broad range of psychiatric and social disabilities which may require a multiservice approach if the patient is expected to function in society. The services may include psychotherapy, family counseling, supplementary education, job training and placement, legal aid, welfare, and other services appropriate to specific needs. While it is impossible for a treatment facility to provide all these services, it is desirable to relate to a network of auxiliary services that can be made available to patients motivated to work with them. This will obviously have to be handled on a trial basis with special services only going to the most motivated patients. This makes for efficient use of services and for the preservation of relationships between agencies.

[12] These are described in Chapters 5 and 6.

A third principle is that the heroin addict comes to treatment from a subculture of addiction which served to reinforce his ongoing behavior and seduce him into relapse during or after treatment. The sociologist John Clausen has observed that to understand heroin addiction one must examine it as one would examine the evolution of a career. Thus, the individual becomes a heroin addict as a result of a complex interaction between personal need and environmental circumstance. Once arrived at, the career is reinforced by a pattern of peer group associations sharing a common jargon, identity, experience, and future expectation which serve to hold the individual to his characteristic behavioral stance. Society, his peer groups, family, and the addict himself all have certain expectations of "the junkie" which continue to shape his behavior much as the certified public accountant is shaped along his own career subsequent to his making a career choice. The heroin addict coming to treatment has a life style which can only lead him back into his addiction. In order for treatment to be successful an alternative life style must somehow be inculcated.

An additional problem has been referred to by the sociologist John O'Donnell who observed that treatment services for heroin addicts are usually expected to prevent criminal behavior. O'Donnell feels that this may be quite realistic in the case of the addicted physician who may be returned to productive medical practice, but may be unrealistic in the case of the heroin addict whose criminal behavior antedates his addiction. Obviously the patient's subculture and career identity influence treatment outcome to an extraordinary degree.

Principle number four refers to pharmacological reinforcement. There have been no "sociological" or "psychological" theories of an addiction diathesis in animals because existing experimental animal models of opiate addiction and relapse can be simply explained using simple conditioning paradigms. Rats who have been addicted to high doses of morphine by daily injection and who have then been withdrawn, will readily re-addict themselves to a solution of opiate drug available in the cage. Rats who have *not* been previously addicted will avoid the opiate solution while rats who have been previously addicted will prefer the opiate solution to plain tap water. Applying this experience to man, it is clear that patients once addicted will readily relapse in an environment where drugs are available. The psychiatrist Abraham Wikler believes that former addicts (rats or men) re-experience the signs and symptoms of opiate withdrawal (in the absence of true pharmacological withdrawal) when they return to an environment in which the withdrawal syndrome has previously occurred. This "drives" the patient to relapse into a cycle of addiction and re-addiction.

Wikler's animal model of relapse behavior is one application of conditioning principles to the understanding of opiate addiction. Another animal model with even wider application was developed during the past decade. Rats and monkeys have been implanted chronically with intravenous catheters and placed in a Skinner box where the catheter is attached to a source of drug. The animal learns that if he pushes a lever he will be rewarded with a dose of drug administered via catheter. If the drug produces a pleasurable response, the animal's behavior can be shaped around periodic drug reinforcement. Thus, certain drugs turn out to be primary reinforcers: that is, they provide positive reinforcement without drive reduction. The only necessary condition is that the drug is administered immediately after the performance of a specific act so that the animal associates the reward with the behavior. Using this model of psychological dependence, all of the opiates, hypnotic-sedative drugs, amphetamines, cocaine, ethyl alcohol, and nicotine all turn out to be primary reinforcers. While all of these substances are not equally reinforcing, one can observe daily patterns of self-administration analogous to the situation in man. It is of interest that major tranquilizers such as chlorpromazine (which are not abused in man) will not serve as reinforcers of behavior in this model. Moreover, animals will not work to repeat the hallucinogenic drug experience and it is rare that one finds daily patterns of self-administration of these substances in man.

The animal model suggests that drugs of abuse which are reinforcing in the self-injection paradigm act rather specifically on the pleasure center in the brain. Recent work with morphine has confirmed that it acts selectively to increase electrical activity at the pleasure center and to diminish electrical activity in the aversion center of the rat brain. These data emphasize the importance of pharmacological reinforcement which is independent of any specific spectrum of personality or sociological characteristics. While these factors may have contributed to the circumstances at the outset of the addiction, the pharmacology of the drug is obviously crucial in understanding the potential for relapse. From a treatment point of view these observations must be understood for they separate heroin addiction from neuroses and character disorders. In the case of the addict, behavior is being shaped by an extraordinarily powerful primary and secondary reinforcer. In this situation mere interpersonal psychological treatment outside of a therapeutic community offers little hope for effecting behavior change.

The fifth principle in the development of treatment services is the need for evaluation. This is an extremely complex task in dealing with an unreliable addict population. Nonetheless, there are certain behavioral parameters that may be readily corroborated by the evaluation team and the clinician. These bits of information are not only important to the evaluator but of crucial importance in the clinical treatment of the patient. The addict should know that those treating him are aware of his behavior and can frustrate his attempts to manipulate the caregiving system. Urine analysis by thin layer or gas-liquid chromatography[13] has already been referred to in connection with the evaluation of detoxification programs. These can and should be applied to all treatment programs. Patients should be required to submit urine either daily or on a random schedule where urine may be checked at least twice a week. This will serve to check the patient's drug-using habits. In general, patients should be routinely screened for opiate drug use and where other drug abuse is suspected, the laboratory should be instructed to look

---

[13] Thin layer chromatography is less costly and more useful for large-scale screening. Gas-liquid chromatography is more accurate and is most useful in monitoring the accuracy of laboratories using thin layer chromatography. Newer techniques using immunoassay methodology may soon be applied which could make some existing technology obsolete.

for cocaine, amphetamines, and barbiturates. Alcohol use should be determined from the patient, his family, and associates. Work history should be determined on an ongoing basis (weekly, biweekly, or monthly) by checking the patient's pay stub or by establishing relationships with employers. Periodic family evaluations may be fruitful. In general, it is a good idea to develop a system which follows all patients weekly in their treatment program at least through the first three months of treatment. Less frequent monitoring may proceed after that time but the frequency and quality of follow-up will differ for civil commitment, voluntary residential, and outpatient treatments and for different phases of a treatment continuum. Obviously, family evaluations and employment status reports are not appropriate for patients residing in a therapeutic community but may be quite useful after discharge.

The principle of evaluation has now been established as crucial in the development of many programs across the country. In this regard, drug addiction treatment is much more sophisticated than other types of mental health care. The National Institute of Mental Health requires that all agencies supported by it submit common intake data on all patients to a central facility at Texas Christian University. Thus, patients in a variety of treatment programs across the country, employing several different treatment approaches, may be compared and their treatments properly evaluated. Moreover, many programs have adopted computerized record systems with feedback into the treatment system for improved patient care and cost efficiency. This has been especially helpful in large-scale methadone maintenance programs where computerized record-keeping, urine testing, and maintenance prescriptions may all be tied together. For smaller programs and other types of treatment, computerized records may not be appropriate. It is absolutely essential, however, that evaluation be carried out and, optimally, by an independent agency. While the NIMH forms are not perfect, they do present a picture of the kinds of data at intake that one might wish to obtain on all patients. It is suggested that members of interested programs consult with the established programs around the country, particularly those in Chicago, New Haven, and New York, on the types of weekly follow-up forms that have been developed.

Principle number six is extremely complex and certain to arouse feelings. All treatment programs developed for the heroin addict and offering any hope of success involve an extraordinary degree of control over the addict's behavior. This may be chemical control, custodial control, or autocratic control as occurs within a therapeutic community. This is a complicated issue politically and morally. One affiliate of the Black Panther Party in a major American city was quoted in an underground newspaper article on the treatment of addiction as follows: "We don't care so much about methadone per se. What we care about is who's controlling it. If the Mayor's program controls methadone the addicts will be turned away from the revolution and toward the pigs; if on the other hand we control the methadone the addicts will be directed toward the revolution and opposed to the pigs." While the author of that statement may arouse many feelings, it's clear that he has hit upon a major principle regarding methadone maintenance treatment. From another point of view most people who complete the treatment program at Synanon never leave the community. This may be good for Synanon; it will lead to an expansion of its program. It's not clear that this is good for these individuals or good for society at large. Data from civil commitment programs and parole programs suggest that patients incarcerated longer and maintained longer in supervised parole tend to do better than those incarcerated for a short period. This finding comes from the most authoritative follow-up study on patients discharged to the New York area from the Lexington Hospital. The author concludes that in fact a strong measure of control may be the crucial therapeutic variable for the heroin addict.

On the other side of the coin an individual on methadone maintenance treatment is generally free from the "hassles" of his heroin-addicted way of life and is able to choose vocational and personal goals consistent with the majority's ethic. These may or may not be satisfying for him (as for the rest of us) but he has this degree of choice. He views his methadone chemical control as the diabetic might view his insulin. A patient successfully resident in a self-help treatment program feels free of the drug control in his life while feeling freer and more open in his ability to interact with other people (in the therapeutic community). It may be, as the author of the Lexington follow-up study concluded, control is crucial. It is therefore imperative that the patient and the community be given choices in the kind of controls imposed on the patient. An optimal treatment program will offer the patient a choice between a therapeutic community and a methadone maintenance program. In areas of high addiction, where the problem is spreading rapidly and cannot be contained with these two techniques, civil commitment may be viewed as a technique to rid the streets of some addicts.

It is unfortunate from a public health and treatment point of view that accurate statistics on the prevalence of heroin addiction are not known. For years the Federal Bureau of Narcotics[14] has been keeping statistics. These statistics have served to support the Bureau's contention that it was controlling heroin addiction. In New York City alone the prevalence of the problem is at least 10 to 20 times the figure supplied by this agency. In the absence of a true case register, it is impossible to gauge the impact of services on existing cases or the incidence of new cases. Case registers in New York City and Maryland have been developed, but these are not sufficiently comprehensive. The development of a national case register must await some national policy on confidentiality of research and public health data because of the risk of prosecution.

Finally, different patients may respond differently to different treatments. Patient typologies do not now exist but with improved evaluation, prediction of treatment effectiveness may become a reality. Suffice it to say, older addicts do better in most treatments than younger addicts and patients with employment skills and little criminal history have a better prognosis than those with poor work history and extensive criminal history. Moreover, patients with close family ties will likely do better in outpatient treatments than patients who are drifters.

[14] Now the Bureau of Narcotics and Dangerous Drugs.

In retrospect these points seem obvious, yet must be considered in developing and evaluating any of the treatment services described in the next chapter.

In summary, the rehabilitation of the heroin addict requires services for the treatment of overdosage, withdrawal, and chronic relapsing behavior. With regard to the latter, each patient's needs must be considered in their total context, including medical, social, and psychological aspects. Motivated patients should be able to receive medical treatment, vocational rehabilitation, and some form of psychological therapy. It is important that the treatment be carried out in such a way that the patient is protected from returning to a subculture of addiction or to situations where he might relapse to heroin self-administration. Evaluation should be mandatory so that programming may be continually improved. It is also important to consider that some degree of control of the patient is involved in all of the more successful treatment approaches which have developed over the past ten years.

CHAPTER TWO

Methadone maintenance and narcotic-blocking drugs

Generally, in psychiatry, it is difficult to specifically categorize treatment modalities. Individual psychotherapy is almost as much a function of the individual therapist's style as it is a function of his theoretical orientation. Methods of group psychotherapy differ widely and reflect not only the style of group leadership, but also the theoretical orientation of the group leader and the characteristics of group members. Often, pharmacological therapies are interspersed with psychological therapies. Despite the difficulties in differentiating and classifying treatment approaches, therapists readily categorize themselves according to their identification with one theoretical orientation or another. This is usually carried out in a climate of extreme polarity and emotion where, even in psychoanalytic circles, Sullivanians and Freudians often detest and denigrate each other to the overall detriment of the field.

The lack of reason which has prevailed in the development of psychiatric therapies generally also exists in the field of drug addiction. All too often treatment programs have been developed in isolation and under the charismatic leadership of a single person whose particularistic approach is seen (by his followers) as the only effective treatment. Where a single treatment approach dominates in a geographic area, other modalities are systematically excluded while patients who do not accept the validity of the particular model offered are deprived of treatment. Where large municipal or State agencies have supported exclusively a "self-help" therapeutic community approach, patients who were "insufficiently motivated" for prolonged stays in such facilities have been deprived of all addiction services short of involuntary treatment. Where some communities have opted exclusively for methadone maintenance treatment through general hospitals, patients who do not fit the narrow criteria of some of these programs have been excluded from any other form of voluntary treatment. Moreover, in this situation, addicts who wish to remain free of all drugs are not offered the opportunity to exercise this option. Throughout the late 1960's, few communities in this country offered addicted patients a choice of treatment, despite the universally accepted principle that treatment effectiveness depends on "motivation."

The polarization which has pervaded the rest of psychiatry would seem to bode ill for any rational development of multiple treatment services in drug addiction. The history of program development in many communities tends to confirm this pessimistic view. Nevertheless, in a number of locations the effort is now being made to improve treatment services by mixing treatment approaches and establishing facilities on a pragmatic rather than an ideological basis. The Federal Civil Commitment Program and the New York State Civil Commitment Program have both experimented with therapeutic communities run by ex-addicts in an involuntary treatment setting. In Chicago, Jaffe[1] has imaginatively employed ex-addicts who were trained in abstinence-based, confrontation style group therapy to serve as group leaders in a methadone maintenance treatment program. Kleber,[2] in New Haven, has also creatively combined methadone maintenance approaches with confrontation style group therapy. He has also been employing narcotic-blocking drugs in a day care psychotherapeutic facility for adolescent drug users. Finally, New York City, which took an ideological approach to drug addiction when Mayor Lindsay first came to office, has now moved to develop a multiplicity of treatment programs out of the offices of the Addiction Services Agency.

[1] Dr. Jerome H. Jaffe has been Director of the Illinois Drug Addiction Program since 1967–1968. He has recently been appointed to a new White House office to coordinate the Federal program in drug rehabilitation.

[2] Dr. Herbert Kleber directs the Drug Dependency Unit of the Connecticut Mental Health Center at Yale.

Although treatment approaches have developed as ideologically polar opposites during the past decade, this trend now seems to be giving way to a more pragmatic and rational development of treatment services for the addict. This implies the availability of a variety of treatment approaches supported by the broad range of social services described in the previous chapter. The need for a multiplicity of treatment approaches stems from the fact that no "cure" for heroin addiction presently exists. Persons failing in one treatment modality may be successfully treated by other methods. While some treatment programs have a greater success rate than others, this may in part be a function of selection of patients as well as a function of overall treatment effectiveness.

Finally, it should be noted that the least effective treatment available is for adolescents. Not only are adolescent heroin addicts the most difficult to treat, but there are ethical and psychological considerations which preclude or discourage the application of some of the existing treatment approaches to the rehabilitation of the adolescent heroin user.

The following outlines the three specific categories of treatment which have evolved in the past decade for the rehabilitation of heroin addicts (the first will be discussed in this chapter and the next two in each of the next two chapters):

1. Pharmacological Treatments, including,
   • Methadone maintenance treatment
   • Narcotic-blocking drugs
2. Civil Commitment
3. Voluntary Psychological Treatments, including,
   • Traditional approaches
   • Confrontation style groups and therapeutic communities
   • Exhortative groups
   • Aversive treatments

PHARMACOLOGICAL TREATMENTS

Methadone maintenance: rationale for use in the treatment of the heroin addict. Methadone is a synthetic narcotic analgesic which was developed by German scientists during World War II as one of a number of substitutes for morphine and other derivatives of naturally occurring opium. It is effective by mouth with a relatively long duration of action. Ease of oral administration and its long-acting characteristics made it ideal in the treatment of heroin and other opiate withdrawal syndromes. These characteristics also account for its usefulness in maintenance treatment programs. In the early 1960's, the Narcotic Addiction Foundation of British Columbia, Canada, began empirical experimentation with low dosage (approximately 30 mg./day) methadone maintenance treatment in response to a high relapse rate in patients who had been detoxified on methadone. Prolonged low dose outpatient maintenance was conceived of as an extended detoxification program which would hold patients in treatment and presumably facilitate transition to a more socially acceptable way of life. Withdrawal from methadone would be determined by criteria of social adjustment rather than medical need as defined by withdrawal symptoms. Patients whose life situation had improved would then be withdrawn from all opiates. The work in British Columbia developed on an empirical basis. The clinicians observed that patients had previously been coming to treatment in order to receive methadone rather than to be detoxified. Using low doses of methadone as a "reward" (or, perhaps, as a tranquilizer), the British Columbia physicians attempted to rehabilitate their patients by holding them in treatment with a self-selected reinforcer.

Proceeding from the research orientation of the pharmacologist, Dr. Vincent Dole[3] of the Rockefeller University in New York began experimenting with high dosage methadone maintenance treatment for the heroin addict. Dr. Dole's work derives from his theory that chronic exposure to addictive drugs (such as heroin) causes cellular changes and other physiological effects which remain after detoxification has occurred. These changes presumably account for the high rate of relapse previously associated with the treatment of the heroin addict. Dr.

[3] In this work, Dr. Dole benefited as well from the clinical empiricism of his collaborator, Dr. Marie Nyswander.

Dole hypothesizes that, as a result of their addiction, heroin addicts are as dependent upon continued opiate administration as diabetics who require an external source of insulin for the duration of their lives. While the diabetic's need for insulin is well established, it is by no means clear that heroin addicts have a similar requirement for opiates. Research in animals and humans at the Addiction Research Center at Lexington, Kentucky, has generally shown that withdrawal from opiates proceeds in two phases: (a) an acute phase withdrawal syndrome lasting from 24 to 72 hours and relieved by methadone substitution; and (b) a subacute period of altered physiology lasting approximately six months and characterized by altered responsiveness to opiate drugs and alterations in blood pressure and other physiologic measures. The subacute phase of withdrawal which may include feelings of "drug hunger" may account for some of the tendency to early relapse following detoxification. Moreover, Abraham Wikler has shown that previously addicted rats will "relapse" [4] for periods in excess of one year following opiate withdrawal. Since the subacute period is presumably over by this time, Wikler has attributed the relapsing tendency in animals and patients to powerful conditioning factors rather than altered physiology. Indeed, while Dole has emphasized the physiological basis for methadone maintenance treatment, it is very clear that methadone (as an opiate drug) is a powerful primary and secondary reinforcer which can be used to shape behavior in socially meaningful ways. At this writing the relative importance of altered physiology vs. psychological reinforcement has not been adequately studied.

Whatever the basis, it is clear that methadone maintenance offers clear advantages over heroin or other short-acting opiate substitutes. There is no euphoric "high" associated with oral methadone administration whereas the intravenous administration of heroin (as in Britain) does cause euphoria. When patients are maintained on high doses of methadone (80–140 mg./day), they become tolerant to most of the side effects of opiates and may function without any psychomotor impairment. They may work without showing signs of intoxica-

[4] See Chapter 1, p. 29.

tion. From a treatment perspective, high dosage methadone maintenance offers two distinct advantages. "Drug hunger" is satisfied in the absence of euphoria or manifest intoxication, and patients are tolerant to any injected heroin so that relapse to heroin self-administration on the street will not result in a euphoric "high." Dole calls this "blockade" and he feels that it is crucial to the success of treatment. Patients maintained on lower doses of methadone (30 mg./day) may experience some satisfaction of "drug hunger" but they are not tolerant to self-administered heroin and will experience a "high" should they relapse in the community.

In summary, the Dole approach offers a two-pronged attack on the problem. If the methadone maintained heroin addict should relapse to heroin use during treatment, he will not experience the reinforcing euphoria and will eventually stop heroin-seeking behavior. Moreover, "drug hunger" is being satisfied, enabling the clinicians to shape the patient's behavior in more socially acceptable directions.

Clinical approaches and new perspectives on methadone maintenance treatment. In their initial work, Vincent Dole and Marie Nyswander utilized a six-week inpatient induction period to stabilize patients on 80–120 mg. of methadone per day. Discharge from the hospital was followed by daily visits to an outpatient clinic where methadone was dispensed in fruit juice, and urine was screened for heroin and other drugs of abuse. When a patient had been in the program for a period of time (generally one year), he could be trusted to take a weekly supply of methadone home with him and return to the clinic weekly for medication and ancillary treatment services. The Dole-Nyswander program, in addition to providing methadone maintenance, also provided some ancillary services particularly in job training and education. The aim of treatment was to stabilize patients on high doses of methadone so that they might be socially rehabilitated. Anecdotal reports from Dr. Nyswander suggested that attempts to withdraw patients from these doses of methadone generally resulted in relapse to heroin addiction. Dr. Nyswander felt that methadone maintained patients were psychologically "normal." Independent psychological assessments, particularly on psychomotor performance, found no deficits. The principal complaints of methadone patients included constipation and occasional over-sedation. The oversedation could be easily handled by lowering the dose.

Wieland, Jaffe, Kleber, and others have modified the Dole-Nyswander technique. The practice of outpatient induction has eliminated the costly six-week initial hospitalization that Dole and Nyswander had required. Wieland, Jaffe, Goldstein, and others have now confirmed that patients can be well maintained on an outpatient basis without the need for initial hospitalization. Some patients do drop out of treatment during the outpatient induction phase, but the overall treatment results are equal to those reported by Dole and Nyswander.

Jaffe and Goldstein have been experimenting with low dose methadone maintenance (40–50 mg./day). They claim that the results of treatment in this dosage range are as good or nearly as good as for patients maintained at higher dose ranges. Jaffe argues that there may be certain theoretical advantages to lower doses relating to fewer side effects, greater eventual ease in withdrawing those patients who wish to be withdrawn and potentially less methadone getting into illicit channels of distribution.[5] There is a slightly greater rate of loss of patients maintained at 50 mg./day, but Goldstein argues that this attrition may be overcome by rapidly inducing all patients to doses of 100 mg./day and then withdrawing them to a maintenance range of 50 mg./day. At this writing the question of "proper dosage" is still unresolved, with Perkins and Block arguing in favor of higher doses (approximately 140 mg./day) while Jaffe, Meyer, and others continue to explore the efficacy of the lower dose range. Wieland who has been studying patients maintained on 25–30 mg./day claims treatment effectiveness with a significantly smaller percentage of patients than the 100 mg./day group.

[5] In many programs, patients take some methadone home with them to be taken when the clinic is not in operation. If patients learn that they can get along on half of their prescribed dose, some may be tempted to sell the remainder on the black market. If patients receive a smaller dose, this practice may be discouraged.

In general, daily doses of at least 80 mg. are recommended for methadone maintenance treatment. While dosages above this level are debated, it is generally agreed that treatment personnel should avoid the dosage question with patients. Dosage effectiveness should be determined by the objective criteria of patient adjustment, urine screening, and manifest signs of intoxication or withdrawal. Pending the development of additional data, new programs should opt for the Dole-Nyswander technique using outpatient induction.[6] New program chiefs should visit established facilities to learn the techniques and options of methadone maintenance.

Finally, there has been some experimentation with alpha acetyl methadol which is a methadone-like substance with a 72-hour duration of action. Utilizing this drug on an experimental basis, Jaffe in Chicago and Blachely in Oregon have been able to reduce the frequency of visits by patients and thereby cut the costs of clinic operation. This drug also increases the potential for reaching larger numbers of patients in any one clinic. Obviously, with the development of longer-acting substances, the need for daily visits to the clinic may be eliminated and more patients may be served.[7]

The Dole-Nyswander program has been evaluated by a group from the Columbia University School of Public Health under the direction of Dr. Francis Gearing. Their report confirms the effectiveness of methadone maintenance treatment but includes specific recommendations which emphasize the need for careful supervision and ancillary services.

New programs which plan to use methadone maintenance should include all elements of the program including: (a) adequate laboratory facilities for

[6] With a starting dose of 30 mg./day, the dose may be increased by 10–20 mg./week over several weeks to the 80–120 mg./day range. In general, administration of liquid methadone in fruit juice is preferred although non-injectable disc-ettes have recently been developed.

[7] If a clinic can currently treat 200 patients on methadone maintenance with daily clinic visits, the introduction of longer-acting drugs like alpha acetyl methadol should permit the clinic to increase its case load 2–3 fold.

frequent accurate urine testing; (b) medical and psychiatric supervision; (c) backup hospitalization facilities; (d) adequate staff to include vocational, social, and educational support and counseling; (e) rigid control of methods of dispensing methadone and the number and size of doses given for self-administration in order to prevent diversion to illicit sale and use; (f) care and selection of the patients to prevent addicting an individual who had not previously been physiologically addicted. Staff members of potential new programs . . . should be trained in this technique in a medical center which has been shown to use methadone maintenance effectively . . . and the combined use of methadone maintenance and other approaches to the treatment of heroin addiction should be investigated.

Finally, methadone maintenance was not considered to be a method of treatment suitable for use by the private medical practitioner in his office practice because of the complexity of service and supervision requirements which necessitate a staff of support personnel not available to the physician in solo practice.

While it is not clear what proportion of the addict population can be successfully treated with methadone maintenance, Gearing found that, of over 4,000 patients admitted to the Dole-Nyswander program in New York, 80 percent could be maintained in treatment. None of the patients who remained in the program became re-addicted to heroin and the majority became productive members of society as measured by schooling, employment, and arrest records. A small proportion continued to present problems of amphetamine, barbiturate, or alcohol abuse. The statistics on social adjustment and prolonged remission from heroin use have been confirmed in programs throughout the country with results ranging from 40 to 80 percent of patients showing significant improvement in behavior. There have been exceptions, but these have generally been limited to programs in which the recommendations of the

Gearing committee were not followed. In general, patients over twenty-five years of age with long histories of heroin addiction, crime, and unemployment have been successfully treated, with the results scomewhat less spectacular in the younger age groups. One city, Washington, D.C., has undertaken a massive methadone maintenance program and, perhaps as a consequence, has recorded the first drop in the crime rate in that city's recent history.

The expansion of methadone substitution treatment programs across the country in the past two years has been an extraordinary phenomenon. The growing heroin epidemic plus the relatively low cost of treatment (approximately $1,000 per patient per year) has certainly contributed to this development. Nevertheless, a number of questions remain unanswered in the midst of this expansion. The question of eventual withdrawal from methadone needs to be carefully considered and evaluated. Jaffe, Meyer, Kleber, and others have encountered a number of patients who eventually wish to be withdrawn from all medication. This option should remain open. The general acceptability of methadone maintenance treatment to minority groups and others would be greatly facilitated if patients could expect eventual abstinence. It may be, as Dole suggests, the community will have to be reëducated to accept methadone maintenance in the manner that insulin is accepted for diabetics. The issue, however, is not so clearly defined in the case of methadone maintenance and further studies under way should be actively pursued to determine what percentage of the addict population currently on methadone may eventually be withdrawn.

The problems and potentials of methadone maintenance have been obfuscated by the attitudes of some persons in the Bureau of Narcotics and Dangerous Drugs and certain individuals within the medical and research establishment. Dole, Nyswander, and others have been subjected to various kinds of personal abuse as well as harassment by enforcement authorities. Under prodding from the Bureau of Narcotics and Dangerous Drugs, the Food and Drug Administration now requires any investigator or clinician using methadone maintenance to obtain an I.N.D.[8] After nearly seven years of clinical experience, this treatment modality can no longer be considered experimental; yet the mechanism which the Federal government employs to "control" the development of treatment programs defines it as such. The Bureau of Narcotics and Dangerous Drugs only closes down programs lacking an I.N.D. This confuses the issue and does not lead to the kind of service system advocated in the Gearing report. At this writing, over 270 I.N.D.'s have been issued to programs of variable quality and control. The FDA has no way of controlling these factors. Federal authorities claim that they have no power to set regulations for treatment across the country. Paradoxically, programs funded by NIMH are operating under guidelines set up by that agency. Obviously, States and municipalities will have to move separately to assure quality control and to minimize the risk of methadone diversion in programs funded locally. Methadone maintenance should only be carried out in certain selected centers (in a given locality) with the controls and ancillary services described by the Gearing committee.

It is curious that the Bureau of Narcotics and Dangerous Drugs initially attempted to block the development of methadone maintenance treatment while its officials have at various times continued to speak against it across the country. After a long delay, the Bureau and the Food and Drug Administration announced guidelines on treatment that would permit the physician in private practice to maintain patients on methadone. This position, which includes a tremendous risk of diversion, contrasts with the enlightened positions of the American Medical Association (AMA) Committee on Alcoholism and Drug Dependence and the Committee on Problems of Drug Dependence of the National Research Council (NRC). These groups argue that "the individual physician cannot provide all

[8] An I.N.D. is an Investigational New Drug Application which a clinical research investigator must obtain if he wishes to study a new drug in a patient or group of patients. The new Special Action Office on Drug Abuse Prevention is expected to encourage the preparation of new guidelines as well as a new mechanism for regulating methadone maintenance programs.

of the services for the various therapeutic needs of the patient. The individual physician also is not in a position to assure control against redistribution of the drug into illicit channels." Physicians are urged to participate in the planning and implementation of public programs in drug abuse treatment and prevention. The contrasting positions of the health oriented groups and the Bureau of Narcotics and Dangerous Drugs would suggest (paradoxically) that the health oriented groups are more concerned about diversion than the Bureau. It is anticipated that the recent Federal reorganization of a Special Action Office on Drug Abuse Prevention by President Nixon will support the AMA–NRC position.

Methadone maintenance treatment is not without its disadvantages. It is an opiate drug and the person maintained on methadone remains an addict. Should he be a medical patient requiring opiates for the relief of pain, there are conceivable problems in providing adequate pain relief because of the already very high dose of methadone that is being used for maintenance.[9] Because the duration of maintenance treatment is still uncertain, it is generally felt that adolescents should not be placed on methadone. Moreover, methadone maintenance treatment should be restricted to patients who are physically dependent upon opiates. Persons who use heroin irregularly and are not addicted to it are obviously not candidates for maintenance, nor are persons who abuse only nonopiate drugs.

The long-term consequences of chronic opiate administration on mood and interpersonal functioning need to be explored and research should continue to determine any effects of chronic methadone administration upon various organ systems. While physicians initially refused to prescribe methadone to psychotic patients, multiple drug abusers, or pregnant women, there are no specific contraindications to its use for these groups at this time. The risk to the fetus appears to be less when the

---

[9] The most reasonable procedure calls for temporary increases in the dose of methadone. Some physicians have given patients pentazocine, a new analgesic which also functions as a narcotic-blocking drug. This latter characteristic compounds the patient's discomfort by precipitating some withdrawal symptoms.

pregnant woman is in a methadone maintenance treatment program than when she is self-administering heroin. The offspring of these patients do show withdrawal signs in the neonatal period which should be handled with low doses of methadone. Newborns of *heroin* addicted mothers show severe withdrawal symptoms shortly after birth and present serious medical management problems in the first few days of life. Research on the long-term effects of methadone upon infants born to mothers on maintenance should be continued.

There have recently been anecdotal reports of existential-type depressions in patients maintained on methadone. This would be expected where patients must adapt to new life styles and shed the excitement of the street hustler way of life. These reports need to be evaluated more carefully, but Kleber has ingeniously dealt with the problem by environmental manipulation in which patients are encouraged to become actively involved in community activities. The ex-addict, with his knowledge of the street, can be a unique community resource; many ex-addicts are verbally skilled and can assume positions of community leadership. Kleber and a few others have also reported abuse of cocaine by some patients being maintained on methadone. This only confirms the observation that methadone is not a treatment for the psychological disabilities or social disabilities associated with heroin addiction. It underscores the importance of providing ancillary services to the addict while he is being maintained on methadone.

In summary, methadone maintenance treatment is the single most important breakthrough in the treatment of the heroin addict. Jaffe has found methadone treatment is far more acceptable to the addict population than residential treatment in a therapeutic community or other treatment approaches. On methadone, patients who were previously unemployed, criminal, and addicted to heroin have become productive human beings. More detailed psychological studies are obviously in order, but the results from a number of centers are truly impressive. Methadone maintenance is not a universal treatment for heroin addiction and is not a treatment appropriate for a private practitioner operating a solo practice. In the context of a broad rehabilitation program with multiple treatment approaches, it is probably the most universally applicable treatment for the heroin addict while also being the least expensive. Further work is obviously needed to clarify questions with regard to risk and the possibility of eventual detoxification while, on the other hand, considerable community education is required to increase the acceptability of this treatment modality in communities with high addiction rates. For the moment, methadone substitution should be restricted to older patients (i.e., non-adolescents) with a verifiable history of addiction to opiates. While preference should be given to patients who have failed in other forms of treatments, this should not be a criterion for treatment.

Methadone maintenance treatment involves the stabilization of heroin addicts on doses of methadone ranging from 80 to 140 mg./day. Treatment has proceeded most effectively when the methadone is administered in single doses under supervision at a clinic or pharmacy. When the drug is not administered under direct supervision, the potential for diversion is very great. Patients should be initially required to attend the clinic six or seven days per week and not permitted to take more than one dose of methadone with them (the Sunday dose). Patients who have been in treatment for periods of four months to one year should be considered for less frequent visits to the clinic (depending upon circumstances and adjustment). Urine should be screened for all drugs of abuse at least two times per week. Ancillary services are needed to treat social and psychological disabilities of individual patients. It is anticipated that longer-acting forms of methadone (or the methadol series) will be developed which will increase the availability of this type of treatment to larger numbers of patients at reduced cost. While changes can be expected, the principle of pharmacological maintenance treatment has now been established in the field of heroin addiction.

Maintenance with narcotic-blocking drugs: Rationale. It is an accepted tenet of learning theory in experimental psychology that learned behaviors may be extinguished by removing or otherwise preventing their reward or reinforcement. When a rat has learned to push a lever in order to receive food, he will continue to push the lever when he is hungry and he can expect reinforcement. Should the delivery of food no longer occur in response to his lever pushing, he will continue this activity for a short period and then stop. In other words, in order for behavior to continue, it needs to be reinforced. As described above, a number of experimental studies point to the primary and secondary reinforcing properties of heroin. Thus, the opiate addict is reinforced by intravenously administering heroin or some other opiate drug. Separation of the patient from his drug, as by incarceration, does not lead to extinction of this behavior. On the other hand, were the patient to be "immunized" against achieving the euphoria associated with heroin self-administration, this behavior theoretically might be extinguished. In short, if you take the pleasure away from the heroin injection the heroin injections would stop. The principle may be readily tested in the laboratory animal but is obviously more complex in man.

There are known medications which block the effects of morphine and other opiate drugs. The exact mechanism by which this occurs is really unknown. Some of these drugs have effects of their own as well as causing blockade of opiate actions, but one of these drugs (naloxone) has no effects of its own and is thus a pure narcotic-blocking drug. William Martin, a pharmacologist at the Addiction Research Center at Lexington, Kentucky, originally proposed the use of narcotic-blocking drugs in the treatment of the heroin addict. According to his formulation, a patient should be maintained on dosages of a blocking drug (cyclazocine or naloxone) which will effectively prevent him from experiencing a euphoric "high" when he self-administers the usual street dose of heroin. The patient will repeatedly attempt self-administration, but the absence of reinforcement will lead to eventual extinction of heroin self-administration.

The initial clinical work was carried out by Jaffe, by Freedman and Fink, and more recently by Kleber. The first drug tested was cyclazocine, a narcotic-blocking drug with a duration of action of approximately 18 hours. Because it was not a "pure antagonist" many side effects were associated with it making it unpleasant for some addicts.[10] The 18-hour duration of action required daily outpatient aftercare visits by patients in the program. The disadvantages of cyclazocine did not prevent its effective use in a limited number of patients. In general, 30 percent of Freedman and Fink's initial treatment group remained in treatment, on cyclazocine, and generally free of opiate drugs. The results of treatment were certainly not as spectacular as the results achieved with methadone maintenance, but patients were not being maintained on a narcotic drug and could therefore be called drug free. Cyclazocine maintenance treatment required an inpatient induction phase because of the frequency of side effects and because of the extreme unreliability of patients at the outset of treatment. Should a patient miss his daily cyclazocine dose and resume opiate self-administration, the treatment personnel could precipitate a painful withdrawal reaction with his next dose of cyclazocine.[11]

The general preference among addicts for methadone rather than cyclazocine makes this treatment somewhat limited for the larger addict population. At this writing, the use of cyclazocine has not been widely explored but has been tested in fewer than 400 patients across the country. Obviously, further work in this area is indicated but has probably been discouraged by the much greater popularity of methadone maintenance.

Naloxone is a narcotic-blocking drug with none of the side effects reported for cyclazocine. A major drawback to

[10] The unpleasant subjective effects of cyclazocine included dysphoria and hallucinations when the dose of the drug was increased too rapidly. Cyclazocine administration required inpatient induction where the dose of the drug was increased slowly over several weeks to a daily maintenance dose of 4 mg./day. Some recent work suggests that the hallucinogenic effects of cyclazocine may be eliminated by a 600 mg. dose of naloxone administered simultaneously or when unpleasant symptoms appear.

[11] If a patient is maintained on cyclazocine he will feel no effects from self-administered heroin, but if he self-administers heroin and is then given a dose of cyclazocine he will experience an acute and uncomfortable withdrawal syndrome.

naloxone maintenance is that in moderate dosage ranges it has a short duration of action.[12] This directly interferes with its usefulness as a treatment modality because patients will readily relapse to heroin use once the effects of naloxone (3–4 hours) have worn off. Under these circumstances patients would have to visit the clinic six times per day since, in most cases, addicts will not self-administer a narcotic-blocking drug on schedule without direct supervision. Recently, Kleber has been experimenting with high doses of naloxone (1–2 grams) and reports effective narcotic blockade for approximately 12–15 hours. He has ingeniously developed an adolescent day care unit utilizing group therapy and other treatment modalities in patients who are being maintained on naloxone. He administers naloxone at the end of the day so that blockade is effective while the patient is away from treatment. While this treatment has not been sufficiently studied in a large enough number of patients, it does seem to have some potential value particularly as an adjunct to other treatments for the adolescent heroin user. Continuing work has been delayed by the inadequacy of supplies available for clinical research. Recently, the City of New York, in an attempt to encourage research with narcotic-blocking drugs, offered grant and contract funds for basic and clinical research in this field.

Current research interest in this field centers around the development of a long-acting narcotic-blocking drug which might be administered every 2–4 weeks by injection. Technology in the preparation of such long-acting pharmaceutical agents is available so that one can anticipate the development of a long-acting narcotic-blocking drug with some optimism.

The work of Kleber suggests that naloxone can be a valuable adjunct to psychological forms of treatment for the adolescent heroin addict. Fink and Freedman found that cyclazocine treatment was most likely to succeed in patients who did not view their daily lives as dependent on heroin. They felt that patients who saw heroin as an ancillary part of

---

[12] Naloxone, when administered orally, is not a potent drug. When given parenterally, it is useful. A long-acting depot preparation of naloxone is feasible and will likely be developed.

social interaction tended to do better on narcotic-blocking drug treatment than patients who saw heroin as essential to interpersonal competence and intrapsychic peace. While their successful patients were not specifically adolescents, this typology does suggest the possible utility of narcotic-blocking drugs in an adolescent population. In this age group, heroin self-administration may still occur in the context of social interaction. Narcotic-blocking drugs may facilitate the extinction of heroin-seeking behavior in individuals with a short history of heroin self-administration. Obviously, much work needs to be done in this field. Long-acting preparations need to be developed and clinical research needs to be encouraged. At this time, the use of narcotic-blocking drugs for heroin addiction rehabilitation is experimental. It is therefore quite distinct from civil commitment, and therapeutic community and methadone maintenance. Yet none of the more established treatments can be recommended unequivocally for the adolescent group. It is in this group, as an adjunct to psychological therapies and social habilitation, that narcotic-blocking drugs seem to offer the greatest hope at this time.[13]

Finally, it is important to differentiate between the use of narcotic-blocking drugs in the treatment of the heroin addict and Antabuse in the treatment of the alcoholic. The alcoholic who is maintained on an Antabuse will get violently ill should he sniff or ingest an alcoholic beverage or food tainted with alcohol. In contrast, the former heroin addict maintained on a narcotic-blocking drug will experience no adverse effect should he self-administer heroin. Rather, he will experience no reinforcement—no "high"—and his heroin hunger theoretically will be extinguished.

In summary, pharmacological maintenance treatment of heroin addiction has taken two courses: methadone sub-

---

[13] Narcotic-blocking drugs can also be used prophylactically (at least in theory) in special populations at high risk such as military personnel at bases where heroin usage is epidemic and among school children in neighborhoods with high addiction rates. Any such prophylactic program will likely require other educational and psychological inputs in order to be effective.

stitution and narcotic-blocking drug treatment. Methadone substitution seems to act by relieving "drug hunger" and by preventing the euphoric "high" of self-administered heroin by the mechanism of cross-tolerance. Narcotic-blocking drug treatment merely aims to prevent the "high" of heroin self-administration. Both treatments owe a great deal to pharmacological research in their development, while their practice demands clinical sophistication and a broad range of supportive services. As in other areas of psychiatry, the introduction of drug treatments has not represented a "cure," but has rather been a breakthrough of the first magnitude which has enabled a group of formerly "unreachable" patients to benefit from psychiatric and social intervention.

CHAPTER THREE

Civil commitment

Drug addiction itself is not a crime. Until the passage of the Omnibus Drug Control Law of 1970, possession and sale of opiate drugs under Federal law were based on Congressional authority to control interstate commerce. A person possessing or selling heroin was arrested for failure to pay a tax. This mechanism was challenged in the Supreme Court by Dr. Timothy Leary. The Court ruled that the payment of such a tax for possession of marihuana was a form of self-incrimination. By extension this also applied to heroin possession. The Omnibus Drug Control Bill of 1970 controls the distribution of dangerous substances through a licensing procedure.

While Federal law never recognized drug addiction as a crime, a number of States did deal with addiction as a crime. Using the criminal definition, the State of California set up a treatment program for addicted prisoners in 1961 through the Department of Corrections. In 1962, the United States Supreme Court (Robinson vs. California) declared the criminal commitment statute unconstitutional and addiction was declared an illness. Thus, in 1963, the State of California changed its penal code. The California corrections program became the first major state-wide civil commitment program obligating heroin addicts to a prolonged, structured, and tightly supervised rehabilitation program. This treatment approach has served as a model for the development of the New York State Civil Commitment Program initiated by Governor Rockefeller in 1966 and the Federal Civil Commitment Program which began operations in 1967 (under legislation passed in 1966). While other States have civil commitment statutes, the programs in California, New York, and the Federal program represent the major large-scale efforts to deal with addiction via civil commitment.

In New York State, the civil commitment approach derived directly from the California experience. The New York program followed on the failure of the Metcalf-Volker program, a voluntary commitment program for addiction treatment. Under the present setup, a patient may be committed by friend, family, or self or may choose civil commitment in lieu of prosecution. Governor Rockefeller's program emerged at a time when there were no specific treatment modalities available to meet the massive problem of addiction in New York City and New York State; voluntary programs such as Riverside Hospital for adolescents had failed; and some success was being reported for probation and parole-based programs described by Diskind and Klonsky. Civil commitment was seen as the only effective way to deal with drug addiction. The addict was to be forcefully barred from his environment and maintained in an inpatient facility until declared competent for supervised outpatient aftercare. In principle this generally meant at least 12 months of incarceration followed by supervised aftercare of 2–3 years' duration.

The rationale for a civil commitment or corrections approach has been most effectively stated by Vaillaint in his 12-year follow-up study of patients discharged from the Lexington Hospital to the New York area: "There are theoretical reasons why addicts may require more supervision than the average psychiatric patient. Addicts tolerate anxiety poorly; they 'act out'; they often engage in self-destructive behavior that is not consciously recognized as self-detrimental. Individuals with such defenses often do not experience a conscious need to change." In short, to treat addicts in a permissive, unsupervised manner is doomed to failure because these patients have no motivation to change. He goes on to state that: "The authoritarian treatment of addiction is beneficial not because it punishes but because it enforces, and hence meaningfully cares about certain of the addict's needs— needs to which voluntary treatment programs can only pay lip service. The average addict does need to remain drug-free for several months before returning to the community; on return he does need a powerful incentive to work; he does need an unescapable non-parental ally for 'external superego' to back up his own impulse control." Without specifically meaning to propose a rationale and structure for civil commitment programs, the three extant examples of this point of view adhere to the approach described by Vaillaint.

In addition to the theoretical support for civil commitment programs which can be drawn from Vaillaint's work, there are certain real and potential advantages to civil commitment programs in areas of significant heroin addiction. Civil commitment is a way of getting the addict off the streets, if only temporarily. Furthermore, Vaillaint and others have observed that addicts who survive into their late 30's often give up their addiction spontaneously, in a process which Charles Winick first called "maturing out." Thus, theoretically, if the patient can be in a controlled treatment situation until he reaches his mid-30's, the likelihood of permanent remission is significantly greater than at an earlier age. If a patient is removed from the streets during his peak years of crime and addiction, the community theoretically benefits from the lower crime rate while he has a better chance to "make it" on the street after he is released.

Apart from the expense involved in chronic incarceration and control, the system obviously works only as well as the rest of the correctional system, and that is usually not very well. The most detailed follow-up studies of civil commitment programs were done in the California program by Dr. John Kramer who was Chief of Research at the Corona Institution. He found that one out of three patients remained in good standing at the end of one year of aftercare with one out of six remaining in good standing at the end of three years. He felt that this modest degree of success was to be considered in the light of the many problems stemming from the repeated incarceration of patients. Kramer observed that the program served largely as an alternative to prison. Many of the same complaints have been leveled at the New York State program begun by Governor Rockefeller.

At this writing, it is too early to determine the impact of the Federal Civil Commitment Program. Suffice it to say, the Federal government is committing patients to the Lexington and Fort Worth Hospitals[1] and following them in local aftercare programs that have been set up under contract by the Department of Health, Education and Welfare. Nevertheless, a recent report by Dr. Robert Rasor, former head of Lexington Hospital, urges that the Federal government get out of the civil commitment business. He urges that the Federal legislation be replaced by State legislation for commitment to State institutions.

Because the California program has served as the model for the development of the New York State and Federal programs, it is appropriate to review the California program as described by Mr. Roland Wood, Superintendent of the California Rehabilitation Center at Corona and by Dr. Kramer. At their best, the New York State and Federal programs have endeavored to approximate the structure and functions within the California program.

Civil commitment in California consists of an inpatient phase at the California Rehabilitation Center and a mandatory outpatient aftercare program including screening for drug usage, counseling in the context of probation and, for selected patients, residence in a halfway house. The law provides for a commitment of two and one-half years for volunteers and a seven-year commitment for those committed following a misdemeanor or a felony conviction. The law also requires that the first six months of commitment be spent as an inpatient. In practice the average first admission usually exceeds one year for the inpatient phase. After release to outpatient status, the patient must remain free of narcotics for three consecutive years or he may be returned to inpatient status with recommitment to a prolonged program. According to Kramer, the outpatient status of the patients can be suspended for any one of a number of conditions including return to drug use, return to criminal behavior, poor adjustment at work, failure to attend group therapy, or association with known addicts or delinquents. Kramer goes on to say that

---

[1] At this writing the status of the Fort Worth Hospital is unclear. It is probably being transferred to the Bureau of Prisons from NIMH.

"the demands placed on the outpatient's conformity to the 'square' role are . . . quite rigorous, although some flexibility is present at the level of the agent-outpatient relationship." When an outpatient appears to be faltering, efforts are made to assist him to avoid violations which may eventuate in suspension of his outpatient status. Nevertheless, it is a strict program and "failure" may be registered which would not be so classified in other programs. The outpatient phase emphasizes careful supervision of small case loads by corrections-oriented caseworkers. The inpatient phase, according to Mr. Wood, consists of therapeutic community techniques applied to patients living in units of sixty. The therapeutic community techniques are based upon the work of Maxwell Jones and Harry Wilmer. Kramer is generally critical of the corrections aspects of the program, but he seems to feel that the Rehabilitation Program is genuine in its efforts at creating a therapeutic community. "Self-deception is changed. For the first time in their lives many are given the opportunity to examine their own motivations and behavior through a community group technique . . . the therapeutic effort is genuine."

Finally, a Halfway House program in the Los Angeles area provides more supervised aftercare separately for male and female addicts. Geis has described this in greater detail. Because of its connection with the correctional system, it is readily differentiated from unaffiliated self-help groups and halfway houses in other cities.

It is obvious that the California program, in addition to being the first comprehensive civil commitment program, is also the most complete. The goals as emphasized by Mr. Wood are primarily societal: ". . . get the addict off the street . . . provide treatment for addicts . . . control them when released to the community . . . return them to the Center for re-treatment if they cannot adjust to the community . . . and provide protection for society." The 16 percent success rate after three years in the program suggests the great difficulty that individual patients have in graduating from the program. With the development of voluntary alternatives to the California Correctional Program in California (such as Synanon and methadone maintenance), there will likely be a significant decline in non-criminal patients being committed to the Corona facility. Kramer concludes that "commitment programs for addicts can be considered at this time as an interim procedure between a totally punitive approach and evolving non-punitive approaches to the issues of drug dependence . . . ; perhaps they will persist as an alternative for those who are not helped by other programs."

At this writing it appears that civil commitment may be justified as a means of holding addicts in institutions in areas where the prevalence of the problem make voluntary treatment and control efforts unworkable. Thus, political authorities in New York and California may be justified in offering a civil commitment alternative to voluntary treatment. In addition to "holding" some patients off the street, others may be encouraged to seek voluntary help utilizing pharmacological and/or psychological treatment approaches. Outside of these two centers of prevalence of heroin addiction, involuntary treatment is expensive, unnecessary, and generally unsuccessful. Here, voluntary programs need to be expanded. The Federal government should, as Dr. Rasor recommends, close down its own civil commitment program and concentrate on the support of community-based services.

Where civil commitment programs may need to be instituted, the example of the California program should be carefully followed. In other words, attempts should be made at rehabilitation through effective use of therapeutic community techniques and aftercare under close supervision by caseworkers with small case loads. The New York State program which began with much publicity in 1966 saw its budget virtually halved in its second year of operation and its programs described as merely custodial. This is a deplorable development. Finally, the tendency in California to commit patients who abuse marihuana (a situation also legislated into the Federal Civil Commitment Program) makes absolutely no sense and only encourages the potential progression to narcotic drugs by persons experimenting with less dangerous substances. In short, any civil commitment program should be limited to heroin addicts and not be extended to other forms of drug abuse.

Civil commitment is an approach to heroin addiction derived directly from the criminal and corrections model. It is not a treatment method but treatment methods, such as therapeutic community techniques and casework, may be carried out with patients in an involuntary context. Because it has been created out of legalistic definitions, the practitioners of civil commitment programs must be rather strict in defining relapse and encouraging patients to return to inpatient status. The built-in lack of flexibility leads to prolonged commitments.

From a slightly different perspective, there is always a tendency in correctional programs to consider society's needs to the exclusion of the needs of individual patients. In this context, programs are forced to expand their list of clientele and thereby assume custodial rather than therapeutic postures. When this occurs, civil commitment programs serve merely as jails with the same high rate of recidivism.

In general, one can only understand civil commitment programs in areas of high endemic heroin use as alternatives to voluntary programs that are filled to capacity. The expansion of voluntary programs utilizing established treatment technologies would seem to be the major priority in the development of services in most parts of the United States.

CHAPTER FOUR

Psychological treatments

Most of the psychological treatments of heroin addiction are founded on the premise that once the underlying problem (or defect) at the basis of the addiction is mastered, the patient's need for drugs will disappear. The underlying deficit or diathesis has been defined in religious terms, psychoanalytic terms, sociological terms, and, more recently, in political terms. Behavioral modification therapies are psychological treatments which do not presuppose an underlying deficit, but presume that the patient has learned some behavior which can be unlearned. Apart from this special form of treatment which will be discussed later, all of the other psychological approaches to the heroin addict presume that some underlying condition has led to drug taking and continues to cause the patient to turn to drugs for solace.

It may appear somewhat surprising that the psychoanalytic literature on addictions is relatively sparse. In the 1930's, Edward Glover, an English psychoanalyst, described drug addiction as a defense against sadistic impulses. He felt that individuals who become drug addicts tend to be fixated at a pre-psychotic level of thinking and behavior. Rado, writing a few years later, saw depression as the painful core feeling in drug dependent individuals; and saw taking drugs as an attempt to ease the pain while inducing a state of elation. Chein and Gerard saw the problem resulting in part from drug availability and sociocultural disorganization. They also identified the use of drugs in adolescence as an attempt to cope with internal drives and external unpleasantness. The drug state was seen as syntonic with the unconscious needs of individual addicts. More recent psychoanalytic writers have postulated that drug choice is specific for an individual wherein the state of regression obtained in the drugged condition is consistent with that person's true level of fixation and internal need. For example, users of heroin and hallucinogens have been described as individuals who suffer from unresolved infantile problems of separation and individuation. Taking drugs is associated with a sense of fusion that temporarily serves to alleviate massive separation anxiety.

Apart from the psychoanalytic point of view, a number of psychologists using standard self-administered psychological instruments have reported high levels of depression and psychopathic deviancy in hospitalized heroin addicts. However, despite efforts by psychoanalysts and psychologists to define a specific addictive personality, there has been no agreement about the precise constellation of traits which defines these individuals and differentiates them from persons who do not abuse drugs. Rather, the evolution of the individual heroin addict is perhaps best understood as one understands the evolution and maintenance of a career. It is a result of individual need and external circumstance. Once initiated, there is a biological component (the pharmacology of the drug) which serves to reinforce drug self-administration. The various roads individuals take on their way to becoming addicts serve to differentiate them; sociocultural expectations and the "need" to avoid withdrawal lead to the rather stereotypical characteristics shared in common by many of the afflicted.

Traditional psychoanalytic and other forms of individual psychotherapy and counseling which have attempted to break the cycle of addiction have generally failed. This may reflect in part the important social and biological determinants of continuing drug usage which cannot be reached by individual therapy. It also may reflect the resistance of impulsive behavior and poor frustration tolerance to treatments which demand a high degree of frustration tolerance and impulse control. Psychoanalytic theory may offer some insight into the psychological determinants of opiate dependence but the understanding is not associated with any significant alteration in behavior. Psychological understanding is important when one considers the application of other more successful modalities to the treatment of heroin addicts. Patients must be understood in terms of their painful affects (feelings and moods) and their adaptive deficits if one is to be successful in rehabilitating them as individuals. It is possible to get to issues of depression and impaired self-esteem with patients on methadone or patients in a therapeutic community. In such circumstances, these issues may be quite important in the total rehabilitation of the patient. Outside of a therapeutic community or a methadone maintenance treatment program, however, psychological understanding does not increase impulse control or adaptive improvement. While individual therapy may benefit non-addicts (i.e. people intermittently using heroin) it would seem to be of little value by itself in the treatment of the hard core heroin addict.

GROUP THERAPY: EXHORTATIVE AND CONFRONTATION GROUPS

The general lack of success with individual forms of treatment for the heroin addict led to the development of innovative forms of group therapy. In general, there have been two types: exhortative groups and confrontation groups. Exhortative groups have much in common with Alcoholics Anonymous. They often have a religious base and, in general, exhort the individual to give up his drugs and "sinful" way of life while aspiring toward moral conversion with the help of the group. Some organizations have, in fact, mimicked the treatment techniques of Alcoholics Anonymous. Some religious organizations have worked with heroin addicts. The most active have been the Black Muslims and various fundamentalist Protestant sects operating in black ghetto areas of major cities. Of more recent interest has been the development of exhortative groups with political affiliations. In Boston, one such group has had some affiliation with the Black Panther Party and sees the problem in political and revolutionary terms rather than in moral and religious terms. It is interesting, however, that the treatment modality continues to be exhortative, using group support. The exact number of people who can be successfully treated with these methods is unclear since statistics have not been kept. A certain number of individuals, however, are able to identify with the value system of the cult and use group support to refrain from drugs. The process is facilitated when these persons at the same time attempt to convert others to the "new freedom."

Of considerably greater theoretical and practical significance has been the development of confrontation model groups in the context of residential therapeutic communities. These organizations have developed across the country, differing in name, but sharing certain common approaches. In general, the differences have been in style of leadership and membership. Most groups tend to form around a powerful authoritarian and charismatic individual. I haven't met all the leaders of these various groups around the country, but those I have met share a burning vision of drug addiction treatment and usually collect one or more successful ex-addicts around them. The analogy to a Christ with a group of apostles spreading the gospel is not unwarranted.

The first organization using the confrontation model was Synanon. Founded by an ex-alcoholic, Charles Dederich, the Synanon organization came into existence in the late 1950's in California and served as a model for other groups. The importance of Dederich's style in setting the structure and tone of the organization is described in his own words in a book by Daniel Casriel, a psychiatrist who was an early and enthusiastic supporter of the organization. "A cult started to form around me. . . . We started to experiment with different forms of verbal communication group therapy. The first meetings were nondirective. . . . I felt that they were limited and really of no value. . . . After the third or fourth meeting it became apparent that the meeting took on a different quality when *I maintained stout and rigid control.* I became inquisitive [*sic*] and leader of the group." In the beginning and throughout the history of these organizations the power of the individuals in control is obviously important to them and to their structured group of followers.

In addition to authoritarian and charismatic leadership, these programs have also experimented widely with therapeutic approaches in the context of a group living situation. They have incorporated seminars in psychology and psychopathology, basic education, and public speaking. In general, they have developed programs designed to improve the individual and group adaptive capacities of members. They have introduced new forms of group therapy such as the encounter group model where intense gut level feelings are exchanged and any kind of verbal abuse may be inflicted on members. Physical abuse is not permitted. Marathon groups have added a new dimension to the encounter group model. Here, encounters may go on for periods in excess of 24 hours and the fatigue experienced by all results in sensory distortions that qualitatively add to the therapeutic experience.

The structure of each community is built upon a rigid hierarchy. The novitiate enters the program living in crowded quarters, carrying out the most menial tasks. He works his way up within a carefully defined status hierarchy to the point where he has an individual room with some luxury items, freedom of movement and authority within the structure of the community. This hierarchy and the movement of individuals up or down within it is an important aspect of the treatment structure. Within the community individuals are not coddled, but rather are prepared for the harsh reality of life. The general philosophical basis for these therapies is a mixture of reality therapy and existential psychology. For good measure, pseudo-psychoanalytic jargon is sometimes thrown in where it is felt that individuals must progress through oral, anal, and genital phases of rehabilitation to the point where they can be responsible for their actions. It is not entirely clear to what degree these latter principles are of value in understanding the nature of the therapeutic process.

In general, each program divides the treatment experience into three phases. These phases may vary in quality and time period from group to group, but in general they seem to follow the pattern described by Ramirez. He specifically structured each phase as a distinct time period in the programs set up in Rio Piedras, Puerto Rico, and New York City. He defined the first phase as "induction," the second phase as "intensive treatment in a therapeutic community," and the third phase as "supervised re-entry into the community."

All therapeutic communities utilizing the confrontation model require the individual to "fight his way into the program." In other words, the individual must demonstrate at a traumatic initial interview (or series of interviews) his motivation to give up the addicted life style. His interrogators are experienced members of the therapeutic community, ex-addicts familiar with the traditional hustles who can confront the patient about his deviation from responsibility. The intake procedure is designed to weed out the unmotivated. It is carried out with the understanding that voluntary residence in a therapeutic community requires a high degree of motivation and willingness to give up the addict life style. It means submission to the value system of the residential group. For this reason, the patient is asked to show concrete evidence of his wish to enter treatment, "to fight" his way into the program.

Upon entering the residential center, the patient usually undergoes a supervised withdrawal from opiates without the use of opiate substitution. At Synanon this means the addict is attended by other members of the community and merely comforted through his physical distress. At some medically run (or affiliated) programs, withdrawal distress may be treated with tranquilizers in order to take the edge off. The aim of avoiding the opiates in treatment is to reorient the patient away from the use of drugs for symptom relief.

In general, most programs require the addict to remain within the treatment unit for periods ranging from 9 to 24 months. The prescribed residential time span varies from program to program. A number of observers have attempted to convey the "essential elements" of treatment within these units, but like descriptions of psychotherapy, they fail to relate an appreciation of the process to the uninitiated. Volkmann has attempted to define five sociological principles essential to the rehabilitation of addicts, based upon Sutherland's and Cressey's work with criminals and Volkmann's experiences at Synanon. These principles are as follows:

1. If criminals (addicts)[1] are to be changed they must be assimilated into groups which have precise values conducive to law-abiding behavior and, concurrently, alienated from groups emphasizing values conducive to criminality. Since our experience has been that the majority of criminals (addicts) experience great difficulty in securing intimate contacts in ordinary groups, special groups whose major common goal is the reformation of criminals (addicts) must be created. 2. The more relevant the common purpose of the group to the reformation of criminals (addicts), the greater will be its influence on the members' attitudes and values. Just as a labor union exerts strong influence over its members' attitudes toward management but less influence on their attitudes toward say, Negroes, peer groups organized for recreational or welfare purposes will have less success in influencing criminalistic attitudes and values than one whose explicit purpose is to change criminals. 3. The more cohesive the group, the greater the member's readiness to influence others and the more relevant the conformity to group norms. The criminals (addicts) who are to be reformed and the persons expected to effect the change must, then, have a strong sense of belonging to one group: between them there must be a genuine "we" feeling. The reformers, consequently, would not be identifiable as correctional workers, probation or parole officers, or social workers. 4. Both the reformers and those to be reformed must achieve a status within the group by exhibition of "pro-reform" or anti-criminal values and behavior patterns. As a novitiate . . . he is a therapeutic parasite and not actually a member until he accepts the group's own system for assigning status. 5. The most effective mechanism for exerting group pressure on members will be found in groups so organized that criminals are

[1] The word "addicts" in parentheses throughout this quotation has been added by the author. [R.E.M.]

induced to join with non-criminals for the purpose of changing other criminals. A group in which Criminal A joins with some non-criminals to change Criminal B is probably most effective in changing Criminal A, not B; in order to change Criminal B Criminal A must necessarily share the values of the anti-criminal members.

While these principles are of heuristic value, they do not adequately convey the "life" of the group and the mechanisms available to encourage the inculcation of a new value system via group pressure. Casriel identified ten distinct therapeutic tools within Synanon that constituted the treatment approach. These included the paternalistic family structure in which conditional love rather than unconditional love is offered to the individual; the initial screening process and intake procedure including the cold turkey detoxification; the indoctrination process in which patients are to understand that antisocial behavior is not tolerated while any form of verbal behavior is encouraged; the principle of status and mobility in which persons work for position within the organization by prescribed behaviors and work themselves up through four stages of status rating; the seminars in which the group is encouraged to participate in philosophical discussions where there is no solution and no right or wrong; the public speaking lessons in which adaptive behavior is further developed; the primitive ritual of the haircut in which an individual is "taken apart"; the fireplace ritual in which a transgressor of a rule is brought before members of the house and is confronted and ridiculed into an open revelation of his offense which encourages the taking of responsibility by individuals for other individuals; the kind of work situation within the house in which the participation of each of the members is necessary for the program to continue in operation; and finally, the group therapy sessions in which individuals are encouraged to participate openly and freely and to engage in self-discovery.

Obviously, the interpersonal processes within the therapeutic community continually generate new methods and discard older approaches. These innovations are not systematically introduced and evaluated and the treatment outcome cannot be attributed to any single method within the treatment environment. From that point of view, Cressey's global concept of a process of affiliation with a group and its value system may be the most plausible explanation of outcome for the individual addict. The exposure to the group with its demand for affiliation obviously causes a kind of cognitive dissonance within the individual which can only be resolved by rejecting the previous life style or splitting from the group. A high dropout rate is the rule in this setting; but those who remain are passionate advocates for this treatment method. Some graduates of such communities are skilled group leaders and are now much in demand to run local drug treatment programs with a confrontation model as the principal modality. Rehabilitated ex-addicts are valuable treatment agents in this type of project and are also sought as speakers and counselors in drug abuse prevention efforts at the community level.

With local and national demands for expansion of services, existing therapeutic communities have been "raided" for experienced (and inexperienced) ex-addict therapists. When the Phoenix and Horizon House programs began in New York City, Ramirez brought several group leaders with him from the Rio Piedras project, and also recruited counselors from Daytop Village and other therapeutic communities in the New York area. At the inception of the comprehensive drug addiction program at Yale Medical School, the initial therapeutic community set up by Daytop Village was created in a most ingenious way. A number of addicts from the New Haven area were sent to the Daytop facility in the New York area for treatment and training while the Daytop facility in New Haven was set up by experienced Daytop graduates. The plan was for the New Haven addicts who had been sent to New York to eventually return to New Haven in order to run the New Haven program. In this way the local expertise would be brought to bear on the problem by the indigenous addicts, while Daytop provided the training necessary for the development of a viable therapeutic community. In Boston, FIRST, Inc., has benefited from the experiences of graduates of the

Phoenix House program in New York, while the therapeutic community set up at the Boston State Hospital was in many ways influenced by a patient who had been in residence at Synanon for a period of time.

Thus, there has been much cross-fertilization across the country. Existing therapeutic community programs have demonstrated they can graduate some skilled therapists and administrators capable of running independent programs. There is now a significant market for these skills and some ex-addict therapists are earning salaries of between $15,000 and $20,000 per year. A major problem in the development of this new cadre of group leaders is the lack of some standardized training program. Moreover, while these individuals have been responsible for the tremendous value now placed upon the ex-addict role, other individuals who have not graduated from these communities are also setting out to develop ex-addict run programs without the experience or the technology learned in established settings (such as Daytop Village, Synanon, etc.). In Massachusetts, in the first year of a State-supported grant program for self-help groups, 60 separate programs were funded at a total cost of one million dollars across the State. This limited figure failed to meet the needs of any individual program, while supporting many ex-addict run programs that lacked the technology or the experience of more established facilities. There is clearly a need for the therapeutic community movement to define the credentials of ex-addict counselors so that the role acquires the stature it deserves, while the community is protected from the activities of inexperienced practitioners. I know of no State which sets standards for ex-addict therapists and administrators. However, with the burgeoning development of therapeutic communities throughout the country, it is clear that such standards are in order. In the present climate, there is a myth about the ex-addict as the only effective treatment agent for the addict. Given that an ex-addict is merely someone who is not currently abusing drugs, these credentials do not qualify as a helping profession. In the rush to develop programs, this has frequently been forgotten. In the absence of a well-integrated therapeutic experience, the "ex-addict" who applies for a job or wishes to run a program may be on "another hustle."

The confrontation model therapeutic community movement has generated a passionate group of followers with a strong commitment to its ideology, and vigorous opposition to pharmacological treatment and substance use and abuse generally. Some of the faithful have been ex-addicts who were treated in such communities. Frequently, some of the most passionate advocates of the therapeutic community model have been social scientists impressed with brief or extended visits.[2] Yablonsky, Cressey, and others clearly fit into this category. Despite advocacy by these polemicists, the therapeutic community model is not without its problems. The Synanon organization in California is well-known for problems of reëntry. Addicts admitted to the organization seem to have great difficulty leaving the community, and Synanon has become a subculture of residential ex-addicts who remain outside the larger society. Synanon has emerged as a commune and now serves many straight individuals who feel a need for community in the relatively rootless world of California.

Other therapeutic communities also have reëntry problems. While these programs have created a new professional class of skilled ex-addict group leaders, it is not clear to what extent other career choices have successfully been made by patients rehabilitated by these programs. If the ex-addict role and career line is the only one available, then obviously the job market is limited and could present eventual problems. Moreover, the role of ex-addict is so intertwined with eschewing the use of all substances that any hint of regression is fraught with hazard for these individuals. The role of the ex-addict is a job; it is a way of life; it is a value system. In few situations are the three so tightly bound together. The role is, therefore, uniquely hazardous. In general, ex-addict graduates of these programs that I have known have been impressive people. They have been valuable organizers of other programs and skilled group therapists. What is unclear is the degree to

[2] In some cases these persons have themselves become members of the therapeutic community.

which other reasonably rewarding roles are available to these people in society, ones taking advantage of their sensitivity to the subtleties of interpersonal communication.

Another problem with the confrontation model of therapeutic community is associated with the passionate commitment of its followers and their belief in the absolute efficacy of the treatment. The belief is so strong that evaluation of any kind is regarded as an intrusion and an insult. The Synanon Foundation which has received all its funds from non-Federal sources has been under no obligation to document the inflow and outflow of its resident population. However, as Federal and State governments have gotten involved in supporting therapeutic communities, they have demanded evaluation data. Where these data have been made available, the results suggest that this treatment modality is acceptable to a relatively small minority of the addict population. On the basis of a limited amount of data from a limited number of programs, it is my impression that the therapeutic community is able to hold no more than 7 to 20 percent of persons who enter the program spontaneously from intake through reëntry. Dr. Ramirez, in quoting the statistics from the Puerto Rican program, claimed effectiveness in the range of 90 percent with patients who completed his program. This is an unfortunate way to evaluate program effectiveness. If a therapeutic community only counts those who successfully complete it, then persons in State and Federal government responsible for reviewing budgets will feel that very few patients are given any service at all. This phenomenon has happened in New York City where the comptroller's office can find evidence for the successful treatment of only 17 individuals between 1966 and 1971 in the Phoenix House program at a cost to the City, State, and Federal governments of five to fifty million dollars. Obviously, these organizations must keep tabs on every patient that enters treatment, and must determine the drug-taking status and mental and social adjustment of every patient that leaves at any stage of treatment. It may be that patients who do not complete the program can successfully adapt to outside situations without further recourse to drugs. Unfortunately, such follow-ups have not been done. At this point, one can only repeat that the acceptability of this treatment to the general addict population appears to be limited; only a small minority of addicts apply for admission to such programs and, of these, only a small minority actually complete treatment. Those who do, appear to be highly motivated people.[3]

In addition to evaluation, one must ask questions regarding the expense of treatment—a sensitive issue which has not been adequately answered by practitioners of the art. In Puerto Rico, Ramirez estimated the cost to be $1,000 per year per patient. Obviously, when his program got to New York City, the costs were considerably greater, well in excess of what would be a reasonably efficient treatment and prevention program. Suffice it to say, programs which are totally ex-addict run will be less expensive than programs involving professionals. On the other hand, programs involving professionals may have the ability to discharge patients when they are ready rather than continuing them in a de facto permanent residential commune as ex-addict counselors or as communal residents.

In summary, the confrontation model of the therapeutic community has been the most exciting and interesting form of psychological intervention in the field of heroin addiction that has emerged in the last few years. It has led to the development of a new class of mental health service professionals whose former street life and recent therapeutic experience make them uniquely qualified to serve a number of roles in the prevention and treatment of heroin addiction. As a treatment modality, however, the therapeutic community approach seems to be acceptable to a limited minority of highly verbal patients. Those who successfully navigate the treatment system seem to be committed to a life course in the ex-addict career and role.

[3] It has been said that these programs hold a disproportionate number of Jewish patients and a relatively small percentage of blacks. Moreover, Spanish-speaking males are said to have serious problems in mixed-sex facilities because of the shame of being yelled at by women and the importance of "machismo" in this culture.

There is a need for a systematic evaluation of all phases of the therapeutic community approach so that all patients are counted (not merely those who complete treatment) and the value of each phase of treatment can be better understood. It seems clear that the problems of evaluation cannot be determined simply by gross observations of drug-taking, criminality, and employability. Evaluation here must consider the more subtle indices of intrapsychic and interpersonal adaptation which should be altered by the therapeutic community process.

A final note seems in order concerning the usefulness of this treatment in rehabilitating the adolescent drug abuser. Obviously, the therapeutic community need not be limited to the treatment of the heroin addict. Unlike methadone maintenance, the confrontation group residential community can be utilized in the treatment of abusers of amphetamines, barbiturates, hallucinogenic drugs, and other substances. There are, however, special problems associated with young adolescents entering such communities. There is one famous story reported in the press which described the plight of a 12-year-old boy admitted to the Odyssey House program in New York. This patient seemed lost in the rigid hierarchy and confrontation tactics of the program and was discharged shortly after his arrival in the program.

As a clinician, I am concerned about the effects of intense, violent verbal interaction upon young teenagers engaged in a sensitive process of identity formation. The effects of this type of interaction upon a fragile self-image and upon later impulse control in the world at large have not been determined. This issue obviously needs further elaboration and research, but there are suggestions that there is an age limit below which this form of treatment is contraindicated. Arbitrarily, I would say that young persons under 16 years of age should be excluded from these programs and that careful evaluation be given before admitting persons between 16 and 18 years of age.

Thus, the two most effective treatment programs for opiate addiction, methadone maintenance and therapeutic community model, are both contraindicated in the adolescent population. Some adolescents may have been admitted to therapeutic communities without reported adverse effects. It is also clear that the psychological effects of this modality upon different age groups have not been adequately studied.

AVERSION THERAPY

The final model of psychological treatment to be considered for the treatment of heroin addiction is aversion therapy. In Chapter 2, learning-theory principles were applied in order to understand the efficacy of both methadone maintenance and narcotic-blocking drug treatment. Aversion therapy is an effort to apply "punishment" as a means of reducing the frequency of unwanted behavior. This is a misapplication of learning-theory principles which have consistently found that "punishments" do not cause behaviors to disappear, but rather cause them to stop temporarily while preventing their extinction.[4] Thus, the behavior returns at a later point with considerable intensity. The most famous advocate of aversion therapy is the author William Burroughs whose addiction to heroin was treated with apomorphine in Great Britain. Aversion therapy has not been attempted widely in this country, and there are no data which support the general efficacy of aversion therapy in any of the drug abuse syndromes.

The practice of aversion therapy is fairly straightforward. The patient is exposed to self-administered heroin which is immediately followed by an injection of apomorphine or succinyl choline. If he is given apomorphine, his heroin injection becomes associated with violent retching and vomiting. Because the apomorphine is paired to the heroin injection, the use of heroin is theoretically associated with an unpleasant experience.

The injection of succinyl choline causes an immediate paralysis of all voluntary musculature including the muscles of respiration. The patient experiences a frightening feeling of being unable to breathe which becomes paired with the heroin

---

[4] Experimental psychologists have found that the effective way to cause extinction of a behavior is to prevent the reinforcement of that behavior.

self-administration. The use of succinyl choline includes some risk of accidental death as well as extreme unpleasantness. There is no evidence that either of these treatments works better than the other. They have been paired to the sight and use of the needle as well as the heroin injection, but there is no evidence that aversion therapy is valid. In general, there is no indication for the use of aversion therapy in the treatment of the addict, although there is a need for the continued experimental application of learning theory principles to the treatment of heroin addiction and other drug abuse syndromes.

DEVELOPING A NETWORK OF SERVICES FOR HEROIN ADDICTION

The past five years has seen a tremendous increase in the use of heroin by the young of all classes and races. In the face of this relative epidemic, a variety of treatment programs have developed which offer some promise for treating a significant number of the afflicted. It is clear that all treatments do not work for all patients. In fact, most treatment efforts may fail with many patients. In communities with a significant heroin problem, there is a need to develop a comprehensive variety of services so that patients placed in one modality who fail may be picked up in other treatment programs. This requires a network of services with structured communication among treatment facilities, centralized data collection and evaluation, and strong leadership at the local level which can forge alliances between the various parts of the network. For the most part, this has not been done except under some programs supported by the National Institute of Mental Health. The significant and notable exceptions in this category include the State of Illinois program developed by Dr. Jerome Jaffe and the Yale–New Haven program run by Dr. Herbert Kleber.

A basic requirement for the development of voluntary treatment programs should be the availability of abstinence-based treatment approaches for all patients who desire them. These should include detoxification, group psychotherapy, job training and placement, and legal aid within inpatient, out-patient, and therapeutic community settings. In particular, pa-tients should be able to choose residence within a therapeutic community, if they so desire.

Assuming that 7 to 20 percent of patients who enter therapeutic communities will complete treatment and that a significant percentage of those who don't complete treatment eventually return to drugs, there is obviously a need for the development of large-scale methadone maintenance treatment programs. Kleber's group in New Haven hypothesizes that pa-tients may require different interventions at different points in their therapy. Thus, at intake an addict with a full-blown ab-stinence syndrome may require a course of methadone main-tenance treatment for an indefinite period while he attempts to restructure his life through group psychotherapy, family counseling, and other rehabilitation techniques. Using this ap-proach to methadone maintenance, Kleber's group has begun to detoxify a small number of patients who had been maintained on methadone.

Patients who fail in therapeutic communities or in abstinence-based outpatient programs (after detoxification) should have methadone maintenance treatment available to them. Older patients who have repeatedly failed with other treatment modalities should be encouraged to start in a metha-done maintenance program. Therapeutic community workers should work collaboratively with other clinicians in order to identify motivated candidates for an abstinence-based residen-tial approach. Such patients should be discouraged from start-ing opiate substitution and encouraged to enter a therapeutic community. At this writing there are no criteria which would match a patient to the appropriate therapeutic modality. For this reason, a network of services is desirable so that patients are not "lost" to the treatment system.

Some clinicians feel that patients who repeatedly fail in abstinence-based treatment should be *required* to receive methadone maintenance treatment and patients who are re-peatedly arrested for addiction-related crimes should be placed in methadone maintenance treatment programs. The issue of compulsory methadone substitution is obviously fraught with emotional overtones. This is a legal issue which is yet to be tested. As an experimental treatment modality (as defined by the FDA), involuntary methadone maintenance treatment would not be permissible under the guidelines for human experimentation which have been developed by the U.S. Public Health Service. Moreover, there are serious civil liberties questions which would have to be faced. Despite these ethical issues, some areas are reportedly experimenting with methadone maintenance treatment as an alternative to jail for the addict charged with criminal acts. Other cities are offering this treatment to incarcerated patients before release. Obviously, there is an element of compulsion in these latter programs, the meaning of which should be decided by jurists.

In general, therefore, every community with a significant heroin problem should have one or more therapeutic communities, detoxification and outpatient abstinence-based services, and a methadone maintenance program. In areas of severe heroin addiction epidemics, civil commitment may be important in controlling the epidemic.

The problem for which there appears to be no satisfactory solution is the adolescent. This is particularly true for the individual who is not yet addicted to heroin, but who occasionally skin-pops or self-administers the drug in other ways. This patient is generally on the verge of dropping out of school and entering a subculture of heroin addiction and crime. These individuals are at high risk and there are few treatment programs that have developed special approaches to them. Residential treatment as attempted in New York under the Riverside Hospital program was a failure. Day care facilities, providing educational alternatives to the existing school system, may help to keep the young adolescent in school and with his family while he receives psychiatric treatment. As in New Haven, there may be some experimentation with narcotic-blocking drugs to assist the individual in resisting a return to heroin when he goes home in the evening. Day care facilities and residential programs should be fruitful places for testing out behavioral modification techniques which have been applied in other settings working with disturbed adolescents. Obviously, much work needs to be done in this area. Innovative educational and recreational therapies, behavioral modification, narcotic-blocking drugs, and varieties of group and individual psychotherapy need to be explored in order to reach this population.

In summary, rehabilitating the heroin addict is a costly process without short cuts. Therapeutic community treatment, methadone maintenance treatment, narcotic-blocking drug treatment, and civil commitment are approaches which have been tried over the past five to ten years with some success in some individuals. Rather specific technologies have developed around these separate modalities and these technologies are important to their success. Methadone maintenance without ancillary services and control of diversion, therapeutic communities run by untrained ex-addicts, and civil commitment programs which are run like jails offer no hope. In the long run, they will be extremely costly to the community as measured by the direct cost of operations and the indirect cost of a continuing problem of heroin use. Well-run methadone maintenance programs with a sufficient range of ancillary services, therapeutic communities run by ex-addicts trained in the principles of the confrontation model approach, and civil commitment programs which aim to treat as well as incarcerate are real contributions and offer significant hope for some control of the heroin problem in an individual community. Obviously, this is not the answer to the greater problems of drug abuse or even the control of the spread of the epidemic. Significant inroads, however, have been made and communities can make intelligent choices about the development and implementation of programs. Private physicians can become involved in the development of programs, but the treatment of an individual heroin addict by an individual private physician or psychiatrist should be avoided. The treatment of the heroin addict is one area where public health care as carried out by institutions offers significant advantages over the individual practitioner. The limited services of the latter do not approximate the extraordinary needs of these patients and may be readily abused by them.

PART TWO

Treating other forms of drug abuse

CHAPTER FIVE

Amphetamine and hypnotic-sedative drug dependence

The extent of abuse of stimulant[1] and hypnotic-sedative drugs is difficult to define. While a significant part of the illicit market has developed from diversion of manufacturers' stocks, there is also an invisible population of abusers chronically maintained (and unreported) by private physicians. Because of the latter phenomenon, an important part of any effort at primary prevention must be aimed at physician education so that a patient's actual use of drugs may be more carefully monitored and drugs not used, except as prescribed. A number of British studies of pharmacists' records have confirmed

---

[1] Broadly speaking, stimulant drug here refers to amphetamine-like substances including methylphenidate as well as various amphetamine preparations and cocaine. While there is no cross tolerance between cocaine and the other stimulants, the pattern of self-administration in animals and the subjective reports of the drug effects in man are similar. Moreover, the same range of adverse effects (psychosis, withdrawal-depression) occurs with cocaine as with the amphetamines.

In this country cocaine is usually sniffed or injected and its use does not result from physician practice (a problem with the amphetamines). While cocaine is enjoying something of a "comeback" on the illicit market, the pattern of usage appears (at this time) to be occasional and intermittent rather than daily. A small percentage of patients who have achieved some measure of successful rehabilitation with methadone maintenance treatment, and other treatment modalities, occasionally self-administer cocaine on an irregular basis. The psychiatric problems associated with intermittent intravenous and intranasal cocaine self-administration are identical to problems of intravenous methamphetamine abuse. In the Andean highlands of South America there are daily patterns of coca leaf chewing which may present problems analogous to oral amphetamine use in this country. In any event, the discussion below on amphetamines may be generalized to cocaine, with the exception that cocaine habituation in this country does not result from physician practice.

the "loose" manner in which many of these drugs are prescribed and the subterfuges some patients use to multiply
their drug sources. Obviously, no physician should prescribe
these drugs unhesitatingly to a new patient but should inquire
about previous prescriptions by other physicians. He should not
write "open-ended" prescriptions which can be renewed on
demand, and he should review these medications periodically
with the patient to assess continuing need. Patients who exceed
therapeutic dosages are usually aiming at intoxication rather
than mild symptom relief.

The secondary prevention of amphetamine and hypnotic-sedative drug abuse involves the physician in case finding. He should respond to demands for "more" medication by
dealing directly with psychological needs underlying the demand. Where it appears that the patient is not using medication as prescribed but to create prolonged states of intoxication,
discreet referral for psychiatric evaluation and/or psychotherapy is indicated. In general, it can be said that where patients are using these medications as prescribed there is limited
potential for abuse.

The effectiveness of sedative drugs as aids to the
anxious patient (unable to cope with specific or diffuse situations) has not been satisfactorily clarified. While these drugs
do reduce anxiety, animal research suggests that drug effects
can interfere with the learning of coping skills because coping
skills learned in drugged state are not transferable to the
non-drugged condition. The interaction of psychotherapy with
sedative medication in man obviously requires much more
clinical research to help clarify this question.

BARBITURATE ABUSE

The exact incidence of barbiturate addiction in the
United States is unknown—in part, because the addicted can
be readily maintained legally by their physicians, a practice
made somewhat more difficult by recent drug abuse control
legislation requiring physicians to review prescribing of barbiturates periodically. Still, it is generally believed that there

is a considerable population of barbiturate abusers maintained
by their physicians and unknown to epidemiologists. Some
nation-wide random sample surveys are being conducted
(sponsored by the National Institute of Mental Health) which
will eventually present a clearer picture of the prevalence of
the problem in this country. The widespread sale of barbiturates in the United States (nearly 4 billion doses sold
legally each year) indicates that there is probably a significant
problem of barbiturate dependence.[2]

Barbiturate abuse is not limited to any single age group
or social class. Alcoholics often abuse these drugs to potentiate
the effects of their favorite beverage. In the Boston area, there
is a significant problem of secobarbital self-administration
among heroin addicts of Italian-American parentage. Some
patients become dependent solely upon barbiturate drugs while
some persons alternatively ingest amphetamine and barbiturates through the day in order to titrate mood and level of
activity. It cannot be emphasized too strongly that the barbiturate abuser is one who ingests the drug to the point of intoxication rather than for sedation or an aid to night-time sleep.
Obviously, the repeated need to seek intoxication with these
drugs suggests profound underlying psychopathology; once
physical dependence supervenes, this adds to the intensity of
the drug-seeking drive.

The state of intoxication induced by the barbiturates[3]
is associated with errors in judgment and accident proneness
similar to that of acute alcoholic inebriation. Chronic habitués
of barbiturates prefer short-acting compounds such as secobarbital and pentobarbital. The signs and symptoms of chronic
barbiturate intoxication include sluggishness, slowed and
slurred speech, defective memory, and emotional lability.

---

[2] In Great Britain, community-wide screening of prescriptions,
and physician surveys have been used to chart the extent of iatrogenic
patterns of use. This is simpler to accomplish with a National Health
Program. It has also been done in this country with the Kaiser-Permanente
Program.

[3] At various times the term barbiturates is used when the refer-
ence is to all drugs of the hypnotic-sedative class.

Diplopia, impaired visual accommodation, and ataxia are frequently observed, along with deteriorated self-care. As with alcoholics, one often finds evidence of neurological damage and mental deterioration in persons who chronically abuse barbiturates over long periods of time.

The rehabilitation of those addicted to hypnotic-sedative drugs involves some understanding of the consequences of chronic high dose administration of these substances. Among the hypnotic-sedative drugs, the barbiturates as a class may be considered the characteristic agent of abuse. It should be noted, however, that abuse of a wide variety of such drugs has been observed historically ranging from bromides, paraldehyde, and chloralhydrate, to more recent preparations (such as glutethimide (Doriden), meprobamate (Equanil), and chlordiazepoxide (Librium)). In general, any of these substances taken in excess of therapeutic range, may result in a syndrome of chronic and habitual intake associated with physical dependence upon and tolerance to hypnotic-sedative drugs. Psychological dependence on opiates, as defined in the monkey self-injection paradigm has been described in Chapter 1 and applies as well to the hypnotic-sedative class of drugs. Physical dependence does not occur within the therapeutic dose range, but when this dose has been regularly exceeded in search of intoxication (and secondary to tolerance) one finds physical dependence.

As with rehabilitation of heroin addicts, intervention in drug dependence of the barbiturate type involves the limitation of disability stemming from the chronic administration of these substances. Medical conditions warranting attention include the treatment of overdosage, withdrawal, chronic relapsing behaviors, and of medical conditions associated with deteriorated self-care and chronic barbiturism. Overdose from barbiturates is fairly common in suicide attempts. It may also occur accidentally when a barbiturate user exceeds his normal dose or mixes alcohol and barbiturates without appreciating the synergism of such a mixture. Unlike opiate overdosage, there is no simple antidote to barbiturate coma. Rather, survival depends on the excellence of nursing care and maintenance of respiration. In some cases, peritoneal or hemodialysis will facilitate clearing these drugs from the blood stream and expedite recovery. However, some drugs (for example, glutethimide) are not readily cleared and present a greater risk. There is a myth among lay people that such comas may be partially reversed by forceful attempts to keep the patient awake. Rather than serving as a treatment, keeping a patient awake merely indicates the level of coma. Failure to waken the patient obviously indicates a deeper coma than one in which the patient is merely groggy. Whenever overdose is suspected, the patient should be brought to a hospital for emergency care.

The withdrawal syndrome usually begins within 24 hours of the last dose and reaches a peak in two or three days.[4] Unlike withdrawal from opiates, the barbiturate abstinence syndrome may result in death and should therefore only be attempted while the patient is hospitalized. Outpatient detoxification (becoming common for opiate withdrawal) is contraindicated in treating the barbiturate dependent patient. The syndrome generally begins with increasing irritability and tremulousness and may progress to hallucinatory states, convulsions, coma, and death. But the full progression is not inevitable. The threat to life is associated with the full-blown abstinence syndrome. A fully comprehensive network of services for drug dependent patients obviously requires some inpatient beds for detoxification from hypnotic-sedative drugs. At various times, the Boston University Out-Patient Drug Addiction Clinic has required 2–3 beds per week for this function. B.U.'s clinic was serving (primarily) heroin addicts from a catchment area of 160,000 persons. Programs treating alcoholics might see many more sedative-dependent patients. Any estimate of the regional need for an inpatient detoxification facility cannot be made on the basis of present information. Suffice it to say, some inpatient bed space should be available in a general hospital for this purpose with staff trained to deal with hazardous complications.

[4] The periods of onset and duration of withdrawal symptoms are a function of the specific drug. Withdrawal from longer acting barbiturates comes on more slowly and persists for a longer period of time.

The treatment of barbiturate withdrawal has traditionally relied on the use of short-acting barbiturates in gradually decreasing dosages. The dosage is arrived at by giving the patient a dose producing a mild state of intoxication and gradually reducing the dose on a daily basis. The need to keep the patient slightly intoxicated appears to be necessary with short-acting drugs in order to prevent convulsions associated with a much higher mortality rate. More recently, David Smith and colleagues in San Francisco have been experimenting with phenobarbital in treating barbiturate withdrawal. They cite the analogy to the use of methadone (which is a long-acting opiate) in treating heroin withdrawal. Their experience suggests the use of phenobarbital in gradually decreasing dosages makes for a smoother withdrawal without the need for a continuous low level state of intoxication throughout the period of detoxification. This is a promising breakthrough which may result in reducing mortality. An additional advantage: at equivalent dosages, the anti-convulsive effects of phenobarbital are significantly greater than for short-acting barbiturates. Introducing this technique has not changed the requirement that all such patients be treated in a hospital.

Treating chronic relapsing behavior is something of an enigma. Unlike methadone use in treating the opiate abuser, there is no relatively non-toxic substance to "block drug hunger" while blocking the effects of any injected material. Moreover, there is no barbiturate antagonist analogous to cyclazocine or naloxone (which have been used with modest success among opiate abusers). Where there is a coexisting problem of alcoholism, some patients have gotten rid of their mixed addiction through affiliation with Alcoholics Anonymous.

The experience of confrontation model therapeutic communities with mixed barbiturate-heroin cases is unclear. I know of several of such mixed addictions that responded favorably to methadone maintenance plus group psychotherapy. There are also, however, anecdotal reports of some heroin addicts shifting to barbiturates once they have experienced heroin blockade on methadone.

In the absence of a more specific technology, one is left

with traditional psychotherapeutic approaches aiming at the underlying problem at the basis of the barbiturate abuse. In general, it can be said that drugs which depress the cortex allow the individual to express considerable affect in the intoxicated state. Thus, alcoholics who appear to be isolated and unemotional when sober will break down and cry or lash out in anger during a drinking bout. The same phenomenon occurs in the abuser of hypnotic-sedative drugs. The goal of treatment is obviously to assist the patient to bear and express such feelings in a non-intoxicated state. In practice this is not an easy task. For some patients, the process is facilitated in a group or family therapy setting. For others, individual therapy, with simultaneous treatment of the spouse, may be more appropriate. In general, the older patient living at home and obtaining his drugs from legitimate sources is a better candidate for psychotherapy than the younger patient who identifies with a subculture of drug abuse and obtains his medication from illegitimate channels.

The literature is replete with single case examples of success with insight-oriented therapy, aversion therapy, and treatment conducted by scholars from the various schools of psychological thought. These case examples are rarely followed up to determine the long-term effectiveness of treatment in preventing relapse. Alas, one is left with an unsatisfying feeling in considering treatment options for barbiturate dependent patients (in contrast to the relative optimism presented in the previous chapters on heroin addiction).

AMPHETAMINE ABUSE

The rehabilitation of amphetamine abusers involves treating overdosage, a psychological withdrawal reaction, chronic relapsing behavior, and adverse psychological reactions to acute and chronic amphetamine use. In general, the amphetamines[5] are stimulant drugs used in treating narcolepsy, neurotic depression, obesity, and (paradoxically) the hyper-

[5] The term is herein used to include Dextroamphetamine, Benzedrine, Methylamphetamine, and methylphenidate.

active child. During World War Two, amphetamines were used to delay or to ameliorate fatigue. This is the most common form of misuse one finds in this country where college students during exam time and truck drivers on the road often use "pep pills" to delay sleep.

There are three other patterns of amphetamine self-administration more clearly recognizable as abuse: chronic daily use to treat the sadness and fatigue of depression; intermittent use for "kicks" in social situations; and use by "speed freaks" who inject large quantities of methamphetamine intravenously in binges lasting 3–21 days.[6] The latter group emerged in the late 1960's. "Speed freaks" are generally young people who have previously used hallucinogenic drugs many times and suffer from depression characterized by nihilism and existential despair. Smith feels these young people turn to "speed" in an attempt at self-medication. A surprising number had taken "pep pills" or "diet pills" earlier in life and generally found the experience pleasurable.

In general, the pattern of intravenous methamphetamine administration approximates what can be observed in the animal model (the monkey self-injection paradigm, page 29). It is a pattern of increasing drug administration over a brief period of time. Eventually the patient tries 1–2 grams at a time.[7] The "binge" is followed by 1–2 weeks of fatigue, depression, and an altered sleep cycle with an increase in dream time. This period is known as "the crash." Smith feels the profound depression associated with the "crash" is the major stimulus to repeated methamphetamine usage. In limited studies carried out in the Boston area, we have found the use of intravenous methamphetamine appears to be self-limited. In general, three years appear to be the maximum period an individual will remain on this cycle (although occasional lapses may occur). A significant number of these patients eventually end up with heroin in an effort to treat the extreme irritability

---

[6] In general, binges do not exceed 7 days unless the person is able to break up the period with occasional 2–3 hour lapses into sleep, allowing him to prolong the episode.

[7] The therapeutic dose is 15 mg.

and paranoia of the high dose methamphetamine reaction. Alternatively this may be viewed as an attempt to relieve the profound depression of the "crash" without resort to further methamphetamine. The "speed freak" has introduced a new pattern of drug usage and new forms of psychiatric symptomatology which have not been observed before. Most of the previous literature on the amphetamines referred to toxic hyperexcitability with oral doses of 30 mg. The "speed freak" who injects 1–2 grams intravenously is obviously quite tolerant to the drug. Users describe the injection as a "total body orgasm"; but paranoid thinking and extreme irritability are also part of the experience. Moreover, the state of intoxication is often characterized by meaningless, prolonged, and compulsive ritualistic behavior. One user was observed standing for hours stirring a pot of spaghetti, seemingly without meaning or boredom. During the binge, eating and sleeping are arrested leading to a state of physical exhaustion which brings the period of drug self-administration to an end. Within 24 hours of the last dose, the patient falls into a profound sleep which may last from 24 to 48 hours. When he awakens he is extremely hungry and often profoundly depressed. Patients should be hospitalized [8] during this "crash" even though there appears to be no specific medical complication requiring attention. Amphetamine withdrawal depression shares the subjective, biochemical, and sleep pattern characteristics of psychotic (endogenous) depression requiring psychiatric hospitalization. Psychiatric hospitalization at this critical time may help to avert a "pharmacothymic cycle" of amphetamine "highs" and withdrawal "crashes."

In addition to withdrawal depression, methamphetamine self-administration can precipitate an acute paranoid psychosis indistinguishable from paranoid schizophrenia. This may or may not continue beyond the intoxicated period and is best treated with chlorpromazine or another phenothiazine drug. The incidence of amphetamine-induced psychosis is much

---

[8] Tricyclic antidepressants take too long to be effective in treating this withdrawal depression which is usually self-limited and seldom lasts longer than one week.

greater when high doses of intravenous methamphetamine are self-administered than when modest doses of oral amphetamines are involved. Amphetamine overdosage responds quite specifically to chlorpromazine (or other phenothiazines), because this group of tranquilizers can "block" the central and peripheral effects of amphetamines.

The medical conditions resulting from high dose methamphetamine usage result from unsterile drug injections (hepatitis, subacute bacterial endocarditis, local cellulitis, thrombophlebitis), malnutrition, crowded living conditions, and inadequate self-care. The hyperirritability of the intoxicated state includes a risk of unpredictable violence, which probably accounts for the motto "speed kills," the public health oriented anti-methamphetamine message encouraged by the counterculture.[9] Chronic users of high doses of methamphetamine complain of difficulty with concentration, and short-term memory (even while not intoxicated). Despite these complaints, we have found no evidence of organic brain damage in 12 patients who were tested; but this may in part be a function of the lack of sensitivity of existing test instruments to subtle forms of brain damage.

The adverse psychological reactions described above for intravenous methamphetamine usage may also occur in populations using low doses of orally administered amphetamines. Withdrawal depression and acute paranoid psychosis during intoxication have been described in this latter population. The premorbid personality of the user appears to play a role in the genesis of the acute psychosis, a function of drug effect–personality interaction. In general, the risk of such reactions appears to be less in this population than among "speed freaks." One adverse reaction occurring in the amphetamine misusers is the breaking through of sleep and/or exhaustion as a function of tolerance to the drug. The reader will recall that this population uses amphetamines to delay the onset of fatigue. Thus, the truck driver who uses these drugs in order

---

[9] Counterculture groups sympathetic to marihuana and hallucinogenic drug usage generally have strong negative feelings about "speed."

to be able to drive all night may find himself suddenly and spontaneously asleep at the wheel. Alternatively he may experience visual hallucinations as a sort of hypnogogic phenomenon.

In summary, the rehabilitation of amphetamine abusers involves the treatment of overdosage, psychological withdrawal, adverse psychological reactions, and chronic relapsing behavior. Overdosage responds well to intramuscular administration of chlorpromazine. Withdrawal from amphetamine dependence does not require specific pharmacological intervention, but the physical exhaustion and emotional depression require psychiatric hospitalization. Amphetamine psychosis is best treated with phenothiazines in a hospital setting.

The treatment of chronic relapsing behavior is an enigma. There is no single characteristic amphetamine problem. The obese, depressed housewife given a prescription for diet pills seems perpetually committed to a cycle of mood and weight change that establishes intermittent prolonged periods of amphetamine intake which she considers "normal" (but which could also be called drug abuse). She eats too much so she can grow fat and be relieved of her depression through diet pills. The person using these stimulants for "kicks" (either orally or intravenously) establishes a pattern of intermittent usage which includes prolonged binges (if taken intravenously) or briefer exposures. In any event, when the period of drug intake stops, depression supervenes. While the "speed freak" appears to be suffering from a time-limited period of intake that may be replaced by daily heroin usage, other forms of amphetamine abuse may go on for many years.

The treatment of chronic relapsing behavior is obviously a function of the population being treated. The middle class, middle-aged person using amphetamines to stave off mid-life depression is best treated psychologically and/or with the aid of antidepressant medications or electroconvulsive therapy which are aimed at the depression. The intermittently obese housewife dealing with neurotic depression is best treated with individual, group, or family psychotherapy in order to break her pharmacothymic cycle. The "speed freak" should receive therapy in a psychiatric hospital to help avert progression to heroin. Jaffe has proposed the use of long-acting phenothiazines in this population. Fluphenazine enanthate has been used in the monkey self-injection paradigm wherein monkeys will stop working for amphetamine injections if the effects of the stimulant have been blocked by pre-injections with a phenothiazine. This is the same principle used in the treatment of heroin addiction with narcotic-blocking drugs (See Chapter 2). Unfortunately, many non-psychotic patients do not like the effect of phenothiazines. Thus, while the suggested treatment has been around for a few years, there are no reported successful applications of it in man.

At this juncture, one can only despair at the lack of specific treatment modalities for amphetamine abuse. Recent changes in the patterns of drug abuse among youth suggest that the "speed freak" is on the wane. The reason is unclear, but active opposition to methamphetamine among counterculture leaders may have played a role. One still finds young people who occasionally self-inject or snort methamphetamine, for kicks; but daily usage or binges are rare. In short, one still finds a pattern of occasional "speed" use associated with a general picture of drug abuse or other deviant behavior.

While the "speed freak" may become less common, the widespread availability of stimulant drugs assures a continuing problem of other forms of amphetamine abuse and misuse. There have been amphetamine epidemics in Japan and Sweden. In Sweden, all use is now illegal. In this country physicians are being asked to cut back on amphetamine prescriptions and there is some consideration of a total ban on manufacture and sale.

In summary, there are no specific treatment modalities for the prevention of chronic relapsing amphetamine and/or barbiturate self-administration. Therapeutic community treatment has not been systematically explored with this population. It would seem to be less appropriate for the middle-aged or middle-class housewife or business man on amphetamines or barbiturates than for unattached and youthful heroin or methamphetamine abusers. Moreover, there is no optimal maintenance drug which reduces the risks of chronic use of amphetamines or barbiturates. There is also no "blocking" drug which can be employed in the treatment of barbiturate dependent persons; and, while phenothiazines do block amphetamine effects, their use in the prevention of chronic relapsing amphetamine ingestion in man is unclear. In the context of psychotherapy, phenothiazines might play a useful role. On the other hand, amphetamine blockade might lead the patient to seek other drugs.

In general, the treatment of choice involves some form of psychotherapy (individual, group, or family) aimed at correcting some underlying problem. It is interesting that the personality differences which might lead one person to stimulants and another to sedatives remain undefined. Thus the psychotherapeutic focus must be defined for each case. Urinary screening for all drugs of abuse and reports from the family on the patient's drug usage are important criteria in evaluating therapy. As we learn more about the natural history of these behavioral syndromes, intervention may become more specific and the evaluation of treatment more systematic. It should be obvious from the above that amphetamines and barbiturate types of drug dependence do not require the setting up of a separate range of services. The acute and emergent medical and psychiatric problems can be handled in general hospitals or mental health centers. The role of the physician should include not only emergency case management but also early case finding and primary prevention through careful patterns of prescription writing. The major priority in the public health approach to these types of drug dependence would appear to be in better education of physicians.

CHAPTER SIX

Hallucinogenic drug abuse

The use and abuse of hallucinogenic drugs in the United States is a relatively recent phenomenon. While a number of substances are capable of causing hallucinatory states in man, only two classes of hallucinogenic drugs have been abused to any appreciable degree. These are drugs which resemble in chemical structure the neurotransmitters norephinephrine and dopamine (the catechole amines) and those substances which chemically resemble serotonin (indole amines). LSD, resembling the indole amines, and mescaline, resembling dopamine, are perhaps the most famous, but a whole range of similar drugs has been synthesized and sold on the illegal market. Psychological dependence associated with hallucinogenic drugs is of a different order than that found in all the drugs previously discussed. Animals will not develop self-administration patterns to any of the hallucinogenic drugs. Moreover, tolerance to psychedelic substances occurs after a single dose and disappears after a few days of nonuse. Thus, daily patterns of self-administration (even in man) are the exception rather than the rule. The principal public health considerations have not been in the treatment of overdose, withdrawal, or chronic relapsing behaviors, but rather in the treatment of "adverse reactions" to the drugs. There is no question that adverse psychological reactions do occur and there has been some controversy about potential genetic damage resulting from the administration of these substances to pregnant mothers. These issues will be described in greater detail below.

Approximately 30 minutes after oral ingestion of 150 micrograms of LSD, an individual begins to experience its psychic effect. Drug-related activity lasts for approximately 8 to 12 hours. The greater changes in sensation, mood, and perception occur during the first half of the experience, while the later drug state is marked by introspection, hypersuggestibility, and, occasionally, paranoia. The psychic effects appear to depend on the age and personality of the user, the setting, the expectations of the user, and the interaction among these several variables.

Jarvik has summarized the reports of a number of experimenters in noting that a change in mood is the first obvious behavioral effect observed under the influence of the drug. These mood changes are particularly dependent on the social situation. States of intense happiness or unhappiness have been stimulated by casual remarks or objects in the environment. Moreover, Katz *et al.* have observed varied emotions in the absence of specific environmental stimuli. Without defining the psychological or environmental substrata, these authors describe three affective conditions resulting from LSD: a moderately euphoric state, characterized by dominant feelings of elation in which dysphoric elements may be present but do not detract from a pleasurable experience; a dysphoric state marked by feelings of jitteriness and tension and a fear of loss of control associated with impaired cognition; and an intensely ambivalent state with strong positive and negative emotions. The latter condition, characterized by intense ambivalence, is the "psychedelic experience."

Apart from these affective changes, subjects also experience initially an intensity of sensory input unknown in other drug states. As the session proceeds, perceptual distortions and hallucinations may appear and there may be a peculiar mixing of sensory input (i.e., smells may be felt, sounds may be seen). When hallucinations occur, they are usually visual, although auditory hallucinations have also been described. Many individuals experience a sense of enhanced creativity and meaning, whereas in fact LSD impairs thought processes and performance. Space and time distortions are common.

Along with the psychic effects, a number of physical symptoms and signs have been noted. Pupillary dilatation always occurs and tremor and dry mouth are common. Moreover, nausea, vomiting, bodily aches, tingling, and sweating have also been described, particularly in persons fearful of the impending experience. Detailed descriptions of the pharmacology and proposed mechanisms of action of LSD can be found in the standard textbooks of pharmacology and will not be described in this section.

The intense affectivity (both positive and negative) and the instability of perceptions under the LSD intoxication can produce states of ecstasy resembling a religious conversion experience. It is no accident that the early groups of psychedelic drug users in the mid-1960's were described by sympathetic observers as being analogous to the early Christians. In fact, hallucinogenic substances are well-known throughout the world and are used in a number of primitive religions as part of the sacraments. However, before an individual is allowed to undertake this personal religious excursion, he is well-prepared by the community through elaborate ritual and not allowed to experience the ritual until he has reached a certain age. In these societies, it is clear that the intense emotional reaction has been structured in the individual and given great religious significance to help the individual integrate this intense emotional state into his world view. The mass marketing of hallucinogenic drugs to young people in this country in the latter part of the last decade ignored the psychic risks to the individual unable to integrate the intense experience. These risks are infinitely greater in the adolescent whose life experiences have not been tempered with age and whose uncertainty (as reflected in an "identity crisis") is often exacerbated by hallucinogenic drugs. It is no accident that users of LSD and other psychotomimetic drugs tend to form groups. Richard Blum has pointed out that the group seems to be a necessary adjunct which attempts to provide meaning to the drug experiences of individual members. Within the group, individuals share a missionary zeal about these substances. In general, once an individual has become a member of such an informal organization, it is more difficult for him to benefit from traditional psychotherapy whose values differ significantly from his drug-using peers.

ADVERSE REACTIONS AND
THEIR TREATMENT

As the use of hallucinogenic drugs reached epidemic proportions in the late 1960's, physicians and street people became increasingly familiar with the adverse reactions and their possible treatment. It has been estimated that the frequency of adverse reactions under controlled laboratory conditions approximates 1 percent while the frequency of adverse reactions to illicit use exceeds 10 percent. The difference is a function of the careful selection of experimental subjects for research purposes by trained psychiatrists and also reflects the fact that these research subjects tend to be older than illicit users and experience a known dose of a known drug in a structured setting. Street drugs, in uncertain dosages, are taken often in unstructured settings by young persons whose psyches have not been screened in advance for the possibility of adverse reactions.

Frosch, Cohen, Rosenthal, Ungerleider, and others have all described a pattern of reaction to hallucinogenic drugs which is psychologically harmful to the individual. Frosch has catalogued these as follows:

Acute reactions. Acute reactions are temporally associated with drug ingestion and are of short duration, being limited to the duration of action of the drug. While all acute reactions are frequently referred to as "bad trips" there are in fact two distinct types of experience, psychotoxic reactions and panic reactions. *Psychotoxic reactions* are characterized by confusion and/or acute paranoia. In this condition the individual may inadvertently expose himself to danger because of feelings of omnipotence or invulnerability. Suicidal behavior has also been reported. In general, this type of reaction is more common where there is inadequate supervision during the intoxication. Most patients who have been observed in this state of confusion have shown poor subsequent memory of the experience.

Panic reactions are often seen at some stage of all LSD experiences. Whereas the symptoms in the psychotoxic reaction appear to be the direct result of the drug, panic appears as a. secondary response to drug-induced symptoms. Patients may show overwhelming anxiety and a fear of going crazy or losing control, with a sense of helplessness secondary to the sensory distortions and powerful emotions generated by the psychedelic experience. In these circumstances the setting, the personality, and the age of the individual and his prior preparation for the experience are important in determining the course of the panic. When complicated by police intervention or unpleasant hospital emergency procedures, the panic may become severe. In a different setting, panic may be a brief moment of dysphoria in an otherwise uncomplicated "trip." Panic reactions are much more common when the drug has been inadvertently ingested.

Recovery from these acute reactions is usually rapid. Most symptoms have usually disappeared within 72 hours. Among groups of drug-using individuals, "bad trips" have been handled by drug-experienced individuals who are at that moment not intoxicated. These groups usually do not medicate the subject, instead preferring the use of environmental supports to assist the person's observing ego to appreciate that this is merely a drug experience. Professionals and nonprofessionals have also utilized phenothiazines (major tranquilizers) and simple sedatives (minor tranquilizers) for the relief of the overwhelming anxiety of the acute reaction. Many persons who have worked in clinics specializing in the treatment of "bad trips" recommend simple support and sedation with minor tranquilizers as the treatment of choice for this condition. David Smith (the founder of the first Free Clinic) feels that phenothiazines, in particular, may complicate an already toxic state. Other clinicians prefer phenothiazines for the treatment of the "bad trip."

Recurrent reactions. Recurrent reactions involve a spontaneous return to the perceptual distortions and/or feelings of depersonalization of the hallucinogenic experience without the reingestion of the drug. These experiences vary in length from a few seconds to thirty minutes. When accompanied by feelings of panic, the reaction is prolonged. In general, flashbacks are much more common in the first year after the drug ingestion and are unusual thereafter. Frosch feels they tend to occur during periods of stress or anxiety while Lettvin is of the opinion that they represent a form of psychomotor epilepsy precipitated by the initial drug experience. At this writing, the mechanism of the flashback is unknown and needs to be elucidated. Similarly, efforts to prevent flashbacks or reduce their frequency by the chronic administration of tranquilizers have been unsuccessful and there is a need to develop new approaches to treatment.

Prolonged reactions. Prolonged reactions include chronic anxiety states and acute and chronic psychoses resulting from LSD administration, but persisting beyond the period of acute intoxication. Chronic anxiety states following LSD administration are probably common and in some cases accompanied by depressions, somatic symptoms, and difficulty in functioning. These states may last many months and are resistant to traditional forms of psychiatric intervention. A small number of patients do develop prolonged psychotic states in the absence of a premorbid psychotic reaction. Some of these psychotic reactions respond to psychopharmacological treatment while others do not. Chronic psychoses in individuals who have shown no previous evidence of psychosis have been observed in persons who have taken LSD repeatedly over short periods of time. These psychotic states have been resistant to traditional forms of psychiatric intervention. While they seem to resemble other types of adverse acute and chronic reactions, a number of psychiatrists have wondered (without documentation) whether these may represent a new form of organic brain syndrome. Up to this time there is no concrete evidence that the use of LSD does lead to organic brain syndromes, but this may reflect the lack of sensitivity of our measures to subtle forms of organic brain disease. In general, most acute psychoses which lead to recovery occur in nonpsychotic, nonschizoid individuals, while chronic psychoses secondary to LSD usage often occur in previously psychotic persons.

Another chronic syndrome which has been described in repeated LSD users (people using 20 times or more) is a depression which has been described as existential in nature. Individuals complain of the absence of environmental stimuli which can give a sense of meaning to life. It is not clear in what ways the depression is related to the LSD experience. Conceivably, it could result from a specific effect of the drug upon the central nervous system. Alternatively, it could be a psychological reaction to the loss of the "idealized self" which is experienced with hallucinogenic substances, but not in the real world. There might also be a sense of loss in the real world resulting from the loss of emotional intensity and the sense of fusion which were experienced under LSD, but not with real people. In any event, this depression has been resistant to standard psychiatric intervention. Smith has postulated that persons experiencing this depression are apt to begin experimenting with methamphetamine in an attempt at further self-medication.

Finally, it is not clear what percentage of individuals who have acute adverse reactions will go on to develop any of the chronic sequelae. However, the repeated use of these substances subsequent to acute reactions seem to bode ill for a favorable outcome. This is contrary to myths among hallucinogen-using young persons who have been told that the way to "work through a bad trip" is to re-experience the drug. In this case, as in numerous other instances, the lore of the street is incorrect and could lead to unfortunate consequences for the individual.

COUNTERCULTURE FREE CLINICS

The rapid growth of large groups of migratory, unemployed, and hallucinogenic drug-using young people in the late 1960's led to the development of a range of services in local communities to meet their needs. As rootless individuals on the run, these young people were ineligible for welfare, traditional public health care, and a range of other services that have developed around the stable, involuntary poor in our nation's cities. Moreover, the distrust with which this group of young people viewed established institutions prevented them from seeking help from established agencies.

The first flowering of this counterculture occurred in San Francisco's Haight-Ashbury during the summer of 1967. Here the full range of youth-oriented services developed that were later mimicked in other cities. There was a switchboard where important messages could be exchanged and where parents could attempt to contact their itinerant children. There was a job coöp in which migratory workers could be assigned day labor activities. There were free stores and free food set up by communal organizations. The message came out of the West about this "counterculture of love" in the Haight-Ashbury and this section of San Francisco blossomed that summer with many young faces furiously dedicated to the counterculture plus various types of hangers-on. These included college kids with the wanderlust and a summer with nothing to do, but there were also more dangerous sociopathic elements who would later increase in numbers and eventually force out the naive young and those seriously dedicated to the counterculture. The arrival of the sociopaths and run-away "teenie-boppers" that autumn was associated with acts of violence and a serious drug abuse problem including methamphetamine and heroin. The worst fears of law enforcement officials seemed to be confirmed in the evolution of the Haight-Ashbury.

While the Haight-Ashbury hippie culture died after a very brief life, the kinds of services that it spawned seemed to be specific for these young people wherever they appeared. Denver, Boston, New York, Los Angeles, and many other cities saw the development of free medical clinics operated largely by volunteer physicians, nurses, and other medical personnel sympathetic to the political and moral message of these dropout youth. These clinics sometimes operated in isolation and sometimes in collaboration with services for runaways. "Bad trip" counseling services were carried out within the clinic or by telephone. The drug-using subculture circulated nationally the telephone numbers of individuals who could be called to take someone down from a "bad trip." A pattern of service developed in the Free Clinics which included birth control information, venereal disease control, the treatment of hepatitis and viral infections and, especially, acute "bad trip" counseling. In some cities, the impetus of the movement for these services developed from within the group of itinerant young people; more often it was the concern for and identification with these young people that drove individual physicians to form Free Clinics and young ministers and theological students to form switchboards and crash pads. In some cities, departments of public health supported the activities of the activist physicians while in other cities the departments looked at the quality of medical care and deplored the separation of these units from more established agencies. One important fact is that the service organizations that grew up within the counterculture had credibility for these young people and they did turn to these facilities for help. In its first year of operation the Haight-Ashbury Medical Clinic saw 30,000 acute admissions.

The problems associated with these informal services were many. Volunteer physicians and nurses readily joined up with an initial flash of enthusiasm to help these troubled young people. The unreliability of the clientele, their insatiable demands, and the routineness of the medical practice led to the passing of enthusiasm and loss of volunteers after one, two, or three months of service. Coverage was not always assured and follow-up was spotty. A part of the Free Clinic culture was the absence of detailed data collection which made follow-up and health screening a difficult problem. The uncertainty of funding limited the range of services offered. While physicians volunteering their time were certainly "establishment" during some portion of the day, they generally avoided referrals to established health agencies and there was clearly inadequate follow-up on patients presenting with "bad trips." Despite these drawbacks, the clinics did make and continue to make a contribution to the health care of this population. They introduced the technique of talking people down from "bad trips" and of using minor tranquilizer-sedatives instead of phenothiazines.[1] They developed the switchboard concept of emergency "bad trip" counseling which has been expanded in many communities to acute crisis counseling centers for adolescents with drug problems. In general, these units represented an idealistic effort to bridge the gap between the counterculture and established society by people who, by virtue of their training, were part of the establishment and, by virtue of their identification, were committed to supporting the viability of a counterculture. The success of this effort varied from city to city. In some areas the identification with the counterculture led to trouble with the local police and public health officials, while in other cities the strength of their credibility to the establishment led to concrete financial support from the city or State public health agency.

As strictly emergency services, the Free Clinics fitted in with the present orientation of the counterculture; but this very characteristic which made them viable in the counterculture was also antitherapeutic and not in the best traditions of medical practice. The founders of these clinics cannot be faulted for their dedication. The services developed were essential. A critique can be aimed only at their failure to establish the principle of continuity of care through linkages with other health agencies and public health education of clients. "Bad trip" counseling, birth control information, and the treatment of acute infections have been the main functions of the Free Clinics. A partnership between these agencies and established mental health agencies might have led to follow-up care for individuals subsequent to adverse drug reactions. The experience of the last five years suggests the need for continuing mental health care for individuals who have had hallucinogenic drug experiences in order to assist them in integrating the "trip" and

---

[1] By checking the quality of illicit drugs, they learned that the market place was full of bogus LSD, mescaline, hashish, and other substances while some substances had been purposely contaminated with strychnine and/or scopolamine. These contaminants presented complex management problems that were best handled without phenothiazines.

going on with their lives. To a great extent this has not been done. Even the adolescent who experiences hallucinogenic drugs without acute or chronic adverse effects should receive some mental health care in order to comprehend and place this intense emotional experience into proper perspective. Free Clinics offering only emergency "bad trip" guidance, and crisis counseling telephone switchboards offering the same service by telephone, contribute to the myth that serious emotional upheaval may be handled in one visit or by telephone. This is unfortunate in that it leads many young persons to disregard the opportunity for help when it might be useful while they drift into a subculture of drug abuse in an attempt at self-medication.

In the area of public health care, the failure of the Free Clinics to establish firm linkages with established health agencies has limited their effectiveness in prenatal care and infectious disease control.

OTHER REHABILITATION EFFORTS

In general, young people living at home and going to school while experimenting with hallucinogenic drugs will respond to individual psychotherapy aimed at some resolution of the adolescent adjustment reaction and some integration of the intense emotions aroused by the LSD experience. Success is limited in persons already showing symptoms of the chronic adverse reactions described above. In the absence of these syndromes, however, the psychotherapy of the hallucinogen-using adolescent who is in school and living at home is the most effective form of secondary prevention in the field of drug abuse. These patients may be able to establish an independent and stable identity without drifting into a subculture of hallucinogenic drug usage.

Once a young person using hallucinogens leaves home and begins to drift from group to group, chances for rehabilitation diminish. Traditional forms of psychotherapy will not affect an individual whose roots run deep into the counterculture. A number of innovative therapists have attempted programs designed to motivate itinerant young people. Their effectiveness is unclear because the natural history of individuals within the counterculture is unknown. The history of the phenomenon is too recent. If everyone who identifies strongly with hallucinogenic drug usage eventually returns unscathed to the straight world, then it is difficult to measure the effectiveness of specific interventions. A number of observers have felt that some people may stay within the counterculture for a few years and then drift back into socially relevant and meaningful life roles, but supporting data are not yet at hand. Certainly, a number of young people have returned from the counterculture and have made an attempt to resume their education and to make use of their greater sensitivity to human need. Others, however, have developed the chronic sequelae of hallucinogenic drug usage or have drifted into the harder drugs such as methamphetamine, barbiturates, and heroin.

The actual phenomenon of Haight-Ashbury no longer exists. Rural communes and urban communes have developed; some use drugs and some do not. These communal living arrangements have an internal instability, particularly when they remain open to migratory youth. The longer-lasting communes have been those which do not become crash pads. From the point of view of the evolution of American society, the outgrowth of the commune as a function of psychedelic drug usage constitutes something of a risk. Some of the finest minds of this generation may have dropped into a counterculture that cannot support their potential creativity—a major loss to society and an adverse consequence of hallucinogenic drug usage. Obviously, in the context of more stable communes, alternative life styles may develop which could further the development of the larger society. At this writing, however, the chances of a salutary outcome are not clear. Where communal life styles continue to be tainted by drug usage, a favorable outcome is less likely. Where group living is an attempt to integrate previous psychedelic experience with positive alternatives to drug usage, one can be more optimistic. This is especially true where commune members are older and have previously established a work identity. Obviously, the development of newer forms of group living represents a complex social phenomenon, not merely a function of psychedelic drug usage. Future events will demonstrate whether individual communes have the stability and strength to endure, let alone influence the larger society in a favorable direction. The outcome for individual "drop-outs" influenced by hallucinogenic drugs will also depend upon the future role of group living arrangements in the larger society and the response of our culture to these new life styles.

The final area of adverse reactions to hallucinogenic drugs is the question of possible genetic risk. Published reports in 1967 suggested that human leukocyte cultures in solutions containing LSD would develop chromosomal abnormalities analogous to those observed in leukemic patients. Attempts to find these chromosomes in circulating leukocytes of drug-using young people met initially with partial success, but the implication of these findings was never clarified. Most viral infections are capable of causing chromosomal abnormalities and this was a population in which viral illness was endemic. Nevertheless, several research workers prematurely concluded there was a risk of leukemia in persons using LSD. This conclusion has since been discredited by controlled studies in man where LSD has been administered to volunteer human subjects without adverse effects in the circulating blood or the blood forming organs.

The observation of chromosomal aberrations in tissue culture did lead to more detailed studies on the effects of LSD in pregnant mammals. Previous work in this field had demonstrated that leukemogenic substances also had teratogenic effects. Several research workers found teratogenic effects in the offspring of pregnant mice and guinea pigs who had been given LSD early in pregnancy. These findings could not be replicated in the rat. Periodically there have been reports of abnormal infants born to mothers who have used LSD during the first trimester. This is an extremely complicated issue because not all causes of birth defects are known. In general, as a result of the thalidomide episode several years ago, physicians usually do not recommend any medication for pregnant women in the first trimester unless it is clearly indicated for medical reasons. For this reason, most physicians feel very strongly that young women who might be pregnant for the first trimester should avoid the use of any medication, especially illicit drugs such as LSD. This is sound advice.

In summary, adverse reactions to hallucinogenic drugs have been the principal public health concern surrounding the use of these substances by young people. In general, the frequency of adverse acute reactions is probably significantly greater in adolescents than in older people. In societies where hallucinogenic drugs are cloaked in religious ritual, adverse reactions are uncommon and generally unknown. The intensity of emotion coupled with sensory distortion (particularly the sense of fusion and the sense of having plumbed some universal or unknown phenomenon) place a severe burden upon the adolescent undergoing the usual turbulence of identity formation. In this situation there is the potential for acute and chronic adverse reactions. Moreover, where there is no ritual or institution in the society to give form or structure to the experience, the adolescent may turn to a group from the counter-culture which may lead to "dropping out" of traditional pursuits and/or an effort at self-medication with the same or different drugs. The uniqueness and intensity of the hallucinogenic experience contribute to a sense of alienation and loneliness which the individual endeavors to cope with through his identification with the "drop-out" group or through the use of various illicit drugs.

Acute adverse reactions can be readily treated with reassurance and minor tranquilizers in settings which serve to reassure rather than to threaten the disturbed individual. Flashback reactions have not been successfully treated to date except through reassurance: the individual is made to understand he can expect these periodically during the first year after his drug experience. Chronic reactions to hallucinogenic drugs including psychoses, chronic anxiety reactions, and depression, have been observed and these have generally been quite resistant to psychiatric intervention.

Emergency services in free medical clinics have developed to meet the medical needs and the acute "bad trip" counseling needs of itinerant young people. In this, the Free Clinics have been very successful. The integration of the "bad trip" (or of any "trip" at all) which might enable the individual to move on in life and away from psychedelic drugs has generally not been carried out, in part because of the absence of continuity of care in established health and mental health facilities. To a certain extent the failure of Free Clinics to recognize the continuing mental health needs reflects the identification of the clinic staff with the politics, values, and life style of the clients. In this context, the individual is seen as part of a movement rather than a deeply troubled human being who is attempting to reconcile a Dionysiac current experience with an Apollonian personal past in an Apollonian society. The failure of continuity of care is a tremendous gap in the system which has not yet been filled. In the areas of both mental health and public health, the volunteer-operated health clinics should establish working relationships with established agencies.

The use of hallucinogenic drugs seems clearly related to the phenomenon of "dropping out." The natural history of this process is still being defined. Certainly some individuals have managed to return to established society while others have sought refuge in Eastern religion and mysticism in an attempt to integrate the ineffable aspects of their psychedelic experiences. The less fortunate have drifted into the more classic drug abuse syndromes with habitual patterns of methamphetamine, heroin, or barbiturate self-administration. The heavy use of psychedelic substances appears to be associated with the chronic use of other drugs. In general, if an individual is referred to a psychiatrist while still living in the home and involved in school, the chances for treatment success using traditional psychotherapy are remarkably good.

Once the individual has dropped out of school and the home and has drifted into the counterculture, he is on his own. Circumstances, as yet undetermined, will lead him on a course through the counterculture to more serious forms of drug abuse, a new life style, or a return to established societal values. The number of individuals moving in any of these directions is presently unclear and is one of the lingering public health questions surrounding the hallucinogenic drug epidemic of the late 1960's. For the most part, Federal funds have not gone to support the services for the voluntary poor who abuse hallucinogenic drugs. Obviously, Federal and local funds are needed to encourage the establishment of a network of services to include emergency health and psychiatric care in informal clinics and mental health centers. Referrals between these agencies must be actively undertaken so that migratory youth are encouraged to remain with a treatment program. In the area of continuing treatment, a number of therapists have tried to introduce Eastern religious studies and visual arts to patients in an attempt to reawaken their motivation toward some life goal. While individual therapists have been enthusiastic about their work, the data that they have collected are at best sparse. The probability of rehabilitating individuals living in the counterculture is clearly undefined at this time and new treatment approaches need to be developed in a climate where they may be objectively evaluated. We have recently encountered some requests for traditional forms of group and individual psychotherapy from itinerant youth living in semiformal crash pads in the Boston area. Requests for traditional psychiatric hospitalization and educational and vocational rehabilitation for these adolescents have appeared along with opposition to confrontation style therapeutic communities. It is alleged that hallucinogenic drug users have been complaining of "sensory overload" which is exacerbated by encounter group techniques. Psychotherapy which aims at clarification and "ego strengthening" has been requested in order to help these young people to integrate the emotional and perceptual inputs of their previous drug experiences. Obviously, there is a need to develop therapeutic approaches to these adolescents which are geared to their present difficulties and which go beyond stereotypes of drug usage and/or treatment philosophy.

Many people are coming to believe that the psychedelic drug epidemic may have run its course and that those who became afflicted are now being channeled in one of the three ways described above. Even if we are at the end of this epidemic, it is important to understand the experiences of the last six years so that if there is a recurrence, we can be better prepared for it. We may then more expeditiously develop services to effectively meet the needs of the population before individual drug users are lost to more serious forms of drug abuse or to dropping out. This is obviously a public health imperative.

CHAPTER SEVEN

The marihuana question

No book focusing on the contemporary problems of drug abuse can ignore the marihuana question. More than any other substance, marihuana (or cannabis) has generated controversy because of the tremendous numbers of young persons involved,[1] the challenge of its use to society at large, uncertainty over the appropriateness of legal penalties, and the unknown long-term risk of chronic smoking. In addition to legitimate public health questions regarding acute and chronic adverse effects and the ethical and mental health implications of felony convictions for possession, marihuana has really become a moral and political issue. For the most part, the political and moral philosophies of those in favor or opposed seem to dominate the formal and informal literature on the subject. One can sum up the current state of the art as the story of the tortoise and the hairs. The long hairs are those who have reviewed the marihuana literature, spiced their commentary with a bit of their own experience and concluded that marihuana is safe, harmless, and more beneficial than alcohol while the law is repressive and wrong. The short hairs are those who have reviewed the marihuana literature, spiced it with a bit of their own experience and concluded that marihuana is dangerous to the individual and disastrous to American society. Tortoises are generally colorless research people who spend long hours obtaining government certified marihuana for research purposes and then report on the acute effects of marihuana in a laboratory situation upon certain rather standard psychomotor and

[1] In surveys of three consecutive classes at a major northeastern medical school, fully 50 percent of the entering class acknowledged some marihuana use.

perceptual tasks. From any single report it is difficult to form a clear picture of the public health implications of marihuana usage. The best reviews of the present situation have been presented by the National Institute of Mental Health[2] and more recently by Hollister.[3] In general there are five general areas which have generated concern regarding marihuana and the public health. These include the effects of chronic smoking on physical health; the question of the role of marihuana in the progression to stronger drugs; the possibility of habituation or other adverse chronic behavioral concomitants or sequelae of use (such as the amotivational syndrome); the relationship between cannabis smoking and crimes of violence; and, the problem, treatment, and consequences of acute adverse reactions to marihuana use including psychoses and panic states.

A number of surveys have noted several patterns of marihuana use in this country. Many persons experiment with cannabis and fail to experience the effects of the drug. This is largely because they have not learned the subtleties of smoking.[4] There is a second group who have experienced the drug effects of marihuana to a mild degree and generally restrict their smoking to group situations. In these settings, cannabis is used in much the same way as alcohol at cocktail parties. The marihuana experience here consists of mild degrees of sedation and euphoria.

There is a third group who irregularly and casually smoke cannabis, and encounter dissociative reactions which appear to be pleasurable. While these reactions can occur in persons smoking alone or with others, this response turns the individual on to his own thoughts whose perceived value far

---

[2] See "Marihuana and Health," a report to the Congress from the Secretary, Dept. of Health, Education and Welfare. Available from the U.S. Government Printing Office.

[3] See bibliography for Chapter 7.

[4] Becker has pointed out that marihuana smoking must be learned and that the perception of effects and their appreciation all require some prior informal educational process. Effective smoking requires that the individual inhale deeply and retain the smoke in the lungs for at least 15 seconds.

exceeds their true worth. Moreover, there is generally some degree of sensory distortion (or "enhancement") including time-sense impairment which usually leads the person to feel that time appears to be dragging. Finally, there is a group of individuals who use marihuana every day or nearly so and seem generally to be seeking hallucinogenic effects from it. This group usually employs other drugs as well to alter internal state. It is my impression that this group is a more disturbed population whose search for "better living through chemistry" has taken them to hallucinogens, amphetamines, and in some cases heroin. They are multiple drug users who eschew the traditional work ethic and find it impossible to make commitment to other people or some life course. Some of this group seem to be suffering from an amotivational syndrome which may or may not include a sojourn in the counterculture. The role of chronic, heavy marihuana use in the genesis or facilitation of "dropping out" is unclear. It does seem, however, that the passive solution to internal conflict, supported by repeated drug use, must encourage this transition.

In the past in this country, marihuana use was largely limited to minority groups in inner city areas. Certain occupational groups tended to favor it, especially jazz musicians and others involved in popular music. More recently, cannabis has spread into the colleges and graduate schools and down to high schools and junior high schools. It is now becoming fashionable among some young professionals in their thirties and forties who apparently long for some previously forbidden fruit of a long-gone adolescence. This pot pandemic has challenged existing laws and law enforcement. The widespread violation of the law and its seeming inflexibility in the face of changing social patterns have obvious mental health implications, especially for the young. Any proposed changes in present statutes must weigh the risk of widespread public violation of the law against increased public health liabilities of uncertain magnitude should marihuana be legalized.

Acute laboratory studies with whole marihuana suggest that for most persons in this setting, acute intoxication is a relatively benign experience.[5] Physiologically, there is an increase in pulse rate (which parallels the psychological "high") and some reddening of the eyes. There is no change in pupil size or blood sugar, although many persons feel hungry during the experience. Time sense is distorted, attention and problem solving are somewhat impaired and there is some loss of immediate recall. The latter is demonstrated by the failure of the research subject to maintain the thread of his own conversation so that he loses track of the beginning of his thought while he is speaking and may compensate by giggling or distorting. Recent work by Jones has shown that cannabis intoxicated subjects are quite inaccurate in perceiving emotions in facial photographs presented on a tachistoscope. While it is difficult to interpret the meaning of such laboratory phenomena, these data are remarkably consistent with gross behavioral observations suggesting that marihuana smoking is an intensely narcissistic experience. Rather than being more "turned on" to other people, the user is really turned inward and uninvolved with others.

Studies using the psychopharmacologically active component of marihuana (tetrahydrocannabinol) have also been performed. A dose-response curve for this substance was obtained by Isbell, *et al.* and by Hollister. At high doses, there are psychotomimetic symptoms similar to mescaline and LSD. At low doses, hypnotic-sedative effects predominate. Euphoria has occasionally been reported at both ends of the psychologically active dose range. In general, the potency of most American marihuana (based upon tetrahydrocannabinol content[6]) would appear to limit the usual informal intoxication to the low dose experience while hashish and certain Asian varieties of cannabis can be associated with hallucinogenic experiences. This may account for the relatively low frequency of acute adverse reactions

[5] This discussion in general describes the effects of smoking. Oral preparations show a delay in onset and the reaction tends to be longer. Moreover, there appears to be a less predictable psychological reaction with a greater frequency of adverse reactions to orally administered cannabis (in contrast with smoked material).

[6] Most "good" marihuana sold in this country has a THC content of 0.8–1.2% while varieties of Thailand cannabis have a THC content of 2.7–3.2%.

to marihuana in this country and the greater incidence of such conditions among American servicemen in Southeast Asia. As the reader might expect, the full range of acute adverse reactions reported for the hallucinogens in Chapter 6 (including panic states, acute psychotic reactions in vulnerable individuals, and flashbacks) have all been observed with cannabis, although with much less frequency.

In general, the principles used in managing acute adverse reactions to cannabis generally follow those outlined in the previous chapter for the hallucinogens. At this writing, the risk of such reactions relative to the number of users is unknown, although psychoses are unlikely to occur in nonpsychotic and nonschizoid individuals. Free clinics which have served the largest number of marihuana users generally feel that marihuana per se is an insignificant factor in the genesis of acute adverse reactions. Factors such as personality, set, and setting are deemed of greater importance. But the philosophy of many of the staff of these clinics is to view marihuana use as a benign form of recreation. This attitude obviously colors their perspective.

Recent reports from the animal and human experimental laboratory suggest that tolerance develops to the hypnotic-sedative (depressant) properties of marihuana while heavy repeated use appears to make the user more sensitive to the subjective experience ("reverse tolerance"). Thus, heavy users show less impairment on standard laboratory psychomotor performance tasks compared with casual users and naive subjects who have been given the same dose of drug under identical conditions. Paradoxically, the heavy user group reports being subjectively "higher" under these conditions than the casual users and some heavy users report dissociative symptoms and emotional ambivalence characteristic of psychotomimetic experiences. Thus, it would appear that the marihuana experience is a function not only of the drug, personality, set, and setting but also of the previous history of use. Recent reports from the biochemical laboratory suggest that tolerance may be explained by enzyme induction. Previously, a number of workers felt that heavy users "learned" how to cope with the marihuana experience thus accounting for their superior performance under laboratory conditions of intoxication. Naive subjects and casual users who had not "learned" adaptive compensation would be impaired. On the basis of present information, it would appear that biochemical changes can account for the tolerance to the depressant effects of cannabis subsequent to repeated usage and that one does not have to postulate the learning of psychological compensatory mechanisms in order to explain the "better" performance of heavy users.

As with other drugs of abuse, therefore, tolerance is observed with marihuana. There is, however, no withdrawal reaction (i.e. physical dependence) when chronic smoking is abruptly stopped. Psychic dependence, as defined in the monkey self-injection paradigm (see Chapter 1) is not known because until very recently there was no way of administering tetrahydrocannabinol intravenously. It is of interest, however, that in North Africa and the Middle East there are skid row populations that remain chronically intoxicated on cannabis. In this part of the world, alcohol is severely proscribed and hashish is the most frequently abused substance. This suggests that unlike hallucinogenic drug usage, daily patterns of cannabis self-administration do occur and could present a problem in a psychologically vulnerable population. It is obvious that a major research question of the next few years will be concerned with the contingencies and consequences of habitual marihuana use. In general, reports from Greece, the Middle East, and North Africa which attribute specific antisocial personality disorganization and/or psychotic symptoms to chronic cannabis smoking must be viewed with extreme skepticism. Apart from differences in potency (compared with marihuana available in the U.S.) these reports are notable for a lack of data on the pre-morbid personalities and living conditions of these patients which make cause and effect interpretations untenable. A recent article written by two Philadelphia psychoanalysts detailing personality disorganization among American adolescents who were chronic marihuana users, can be similarly criticized. Nevertheless, it is important that physicians continue to report possible psychiatric syndromes specific to chronic use of marihuana. McGlothlin has been concerned about the amotivational syndrome among youthful habitués. He fears the loss of aggressiveness associated with marihuana intoxication is reflected in a loss of drive and consequent dropping out. The risks of such an outcome are infinitely greater in the young who have not completed their education than in older users who can later resume careers. While one's view of this phenomenon is colored by one's value system, it is clear that this result is alien to Western man. It presents the habituated adolescent with serious adaptive problems. In general, the "dropping out" phenomenon seems to be largely limited to heavy marihuana users who have invariably used hallucinogens and other drugs. Thus, the specific role of marihuana in the etiology of this phenomenon is unknown.

One argument advanced by opponents of marihuana legalization is that pot leads inexorably to other drugs and eventually to heroin. Retrospective reports of heroin addicts admitted to the Lexington Hospital generally found that the vast majority had used marihuana before moving on to harder drugs. These statistics have been used to support the "progression hypothesis." Most pharmacologists argue that there is no biological reason for an individual to progress to harder drugs. Other studies of patterns of drug use among ghetto youth have found that the vast majority of marihuana users do not use heroin and that some heroin users did not use marihuana before experimenting with heroin. Moreover, the pot pandemic has found multiple drug use among only 6–10 percent of marihuana users.[7] In general, the degree of multiple drug use correlated with the frequency of marihuana smoking. The data suggest a group of persons who are at special risk of multiple drug abuse stemming from serious psychological problems. There does not seem to be an inexorable progression from experimentation to casual use of marihuana into more serious drug abuse syndromes.

In support of the need for anti-marihuana legislation in the late 1930's, Congress heard testimony attributing crimes

[7] College student surveys conducted in the late 1960's generally confirmed marihuana use among 50 percent of students with hallucinogenic use at 3–6 percent.

of violence to cannabis use. Legend in the Middle East also attributed hashish smoking to violent acts. Observers of cannabis intoxication in the laboratory and in more informal surroundings have noted an extreme passivity and emotional withdrawal which would seem to make violent activity impossible. In general, there is no evidence to support any relationship between marihuana and violent crime. Obviously with groups as diverse as "flower children" and Hell's Angels using hashish and other forms of cannabis, varieties of behavior may be observed which can be directly related to the personality and previous aggressive history of the user. Most observers agree that alcohol and other cortical depressants are much more likely to "release" aggression than marihuana.

With regard to chronic physical abnormalities resulting from marihuana use, there have been reports of chronic bronchitis and secondary lung disease in countries where heavy use of hashish has been known for many years. Recent evidence that tetrahydrocannabinol is metabolized by liver enzymes requires detailed studies of the effects of marihuana upon liver function, as well as kidney, cardiac, and brain function. Chronic animal toxicity studies of tetrahydrocannabinol are being sponsored by the National Institute of Mental Health. These studies in two species are similar to work which drug companies are required to perform on drugs before they are released to the public. Recently, the Food and Drug Administration cleared acute and subacute studies with tetrahydrocannabinol in man. It is expected that over the next year, permission for chronic studies will be granted so that the public and the medical profession can get a clearer picture of the potential safety or risk of chronic cannabis administration.

For the moment, there remain serious gaps in our knowledge with regard to the mental health and public health implications of chronic marihuana use. For the most part, single dose laboratory studies and informal social administration of doses of cannabis available in this country appears to be a reasonably benign experience. Moreover, many people apparently smoke one or more times without ever experiencing the effects of the drug. More potent preparations pose a greater threat of acute adverse reactions analogous to untoward experiences with more potent hallucinogenic drugs. In addition, some of the material sold on the street as marihuana has been adulterated with other drugs which may pose a serious threat to the user. It may be several years before the extent of risk can be fully defined. This country has a long history of alcohol use and considerable experience in documenting the tremendous public health risks involved for five million problem drinkers. Moreover, as a nation, we only recently discovered the tremendous public health risks involved in widespread cigarette smoking. The link-up of lung cancer and heart disease with smoking was only clear after many people had been smoking heavily for at least 25 years. The widespread use of marihuana is less than ten years old. It has been a time of massive social change in a nation undergoing wrenching conflict. In this situation, traditional values have been discredited, as the young have attempted to define new styles of living. In a time of massive social change and experimentation, the specific psychological risks that might be associated with marihuana use are difficult to define. The widespread use of all drugs has been in part symptomatic of our social upheaval. Obviously, a substance like marihuana, with elusive chameleon-like effects, fulfills the projective fantasies of both those who seek liberation in, and those who fear, the changes which are happening.

In this situation, the public health approach is unclear. Tertiary prevention seems unwarranted in the absence of some specific symptom complex requiring amelioration. Secondary prevention of more serious drug abuse syndromes could involve case selection among those persons using marihuana who also experience serious emotional problems. This is a high risk group which would benefit from traditional psychotherapy. In this situation marihuana use cannot be the central focus of treatment; while on the other hand, the therapist would do well to counsel against daily use and/or experimentation with harder drugs. In general, most patients accept this advice without defensiveness. It is best to avoid discussion of the relative merits of alcohol and marihuana but rather to focus on the extant public health questions that generate some reason for caution.

Above all, it is unwise to identify either with the "rebellion" of the adolescent or the myths of the parents that their child is "on dope."

Primary prevention presents the greatest challenge. Marihuana use per se is now a function of the environment more than intrapsychic need. It is everywhere, and the vast majority of adolescents will be challenged to try it. With such compelling social pressures, we lack techniques to prevent self-experimentation. Scare tactics generate fears that could precipitate acute adverse reactions even in the absence of pharmacological effects. Any education program must deal objectively with questions about marihuana and might counsel the young against use on the grounds of uncertain mental and physical risk. On the other hand, as marihuana smoking becomes as prevalent as drinking among young persons, we may be approaching a time when the message should be moderation rather than abstinence. This appears to be the lesson we have learned with alcohol, and it may some day apply here as well. One thing is clear. Nearly every teenager knows the effects of marihuana from personal experience or from friends. Thus, it is important to find out the kinds of information he has so that counseling on other drugs (and marihuana) will be credible.

One approach to primary prevention tried by the National Institute of Mental Health in television spots has been the warning about legal penalties. While this is a powerful message, too many people know too many other people who violate this particular law without getting caught. Furthermore, the penalties in some States are so severe that conviction is rare. Commitment for treatment for marihuana use is usually a farce. The civil commitment program in California has previously treated such users on the same basis as heroin addicts.[8] Obviously, this is inappropriate. A number of States have altered penalties for possession from felonies to misdemeanors. Some States are considering noncriminal penalties analogous to traffic fines. The current situation with millions of people failing to respect the law tends to undermine the fabric of society, while

[8] This was true even to the point of requiring periodic Nalorphine testing which would not have given evidence of marihuana use.

making felons of many otherwise innocent young people. Some localities have used these laws to punish "undesirable elements" who would otherwise escape conviction. This should not be allowed to continue.

One recent proposal suggested legalizing marihuana through a licensing arrangement analogous to the State liquor stores in various parts of the country. There are advantages to this proposal in controlling the quality and potency of material as well as restricting the age of the customers. Such an arrangement in advance of additional data on the risks of chronic usage is, I believe, not warranted at this time. A major change in the penalty structure at present could permit public health inquiry to proceed without some of the current urgency. If it is found that marihuana is indeed a safe intoxicant for the individual (and for this society), legalization through licensing would be appropriate.

Any change in the legal status of marihuana users poses a potential risk to society should it result in a larger number of people becoming involved and proportionally more young persons using the substance daily and experimenting with harder drugs. It is obvious from the preceding discussion that I believe such risks are much less than the damage done by the present penalty structure. There is sufficient evidence to warrant changes in the law, short of legalization. The question now is in the political arena. The public health questions of legalization are being defined in the experimental laboratory and in the informal settings where marihuana use is widespread. Moving the focus of law enforcement and public attention away from marihuana and on to heroin and other drugs would have a salutary effect on the efficacy of drug traffic control while turning off the unsatisfying arguments on the relative safety of marihuana and the "hypocrisy" of the law. Focusing public concern upon clearly "villainous" drugs would take the "noise" out of the public health message in this area.

PART THREE

A public health approach

CHAPTER EIGHT

Prospects for a public health approach

What are the prospects for a public health approach in the United States to complex problems associated with drugs of abuse? Given the expense of a large-scale undertaking, does it make sense to launch such a program in the face of other compelling national priorities? On the other hand, with the reality of the present epidemic (including an estimated 5–10 percent of returning Vietnam veterans), can we fail to deal with the problem? Obviously, in a system such as ours with many countervailing pressures there will be various positions taken: those advocating a greater enforcement role; those advocating greater attempts to eradicate the socio-psychological and socio-economic "causes" of the problem; and those calling for a narrow medical solution to aspects of drug dependence which can be dealt with by physicians. The preceding chapters have tended to overemphasize the treatment approaches and medical consequences of various drug abuse syndromes. It is appropriate at this time to repeat the message of the Introduction: that the problem of drug abuse requires not only consideration of medical implications, but also significant improvements in the role of law enforcement in controlling drug traffic as well as efforts to make education and other primary prevention techniques more effective. Finally, it demands some programs attempting to deal with the social conditions in the areas where drug addiction is most prevalent—even though elimination of poverty, hunger, and slums will not eliminate drug addiction from our national life. The spread of heroin among middle class youth and American soldiers has dramatically demonstrated that drug use is not merely an escape for lower socio-economic groups. Programs designed to improve the quality of life among the poor must be considered in their own right and not as programs for the prevention of drug abuse. On the other hand, any mitigation of the heroin traffic among the poor would eliminate a major source of economic parasitism in the community while preserving the youth in these areas so they might become actively involved in changing the external environment instead of escaping passively to an internal nirvana.

The prospects for implementing a public health approach to drug dependence ultimately depend upon the coordination of resources at many levels of government. Until the formation in June 1971 of the Special Action Office on Drug Abuse Prevention in the White House, Federal support programs for drug abuse prevention and rehabilitation were fragmented. At the local level this resulted in the establishment of costly and non-compatible health care systems often based on large, but short-term, Federal financial commitments. The cost of this inefficiency precluded effective implementation of financial resources at the Federal level and treatment resources at the local level. It was more costly also in an indirect way because services set up in this manner are doomed since much time must be spent recruiting funds to sustain a treatment effort that is, of necessity, long-term in nature. Treatment staff have been burdened by the need to obtain money, while facing the demands of a difficult patient population and unreasonable political forces in many communities. The extraordinary emotional demands on persons setting up community-based treatment facilities has led to a situation where only the strong or the masochistic seek out such positions, and even then remain only 2–3 years.

Drug abuse treatment facilities require long-term, flexible, financial support, programmatic adaptability to meet the complex needs of individual patients and their families, coordination with various agencies, and long and short-term evaluation. In order for this camelot to exist at the local level, these qualities must be reflected in Federal legislation and the regulations of funding agencies. Until the recent establishment of the Special Action Office, Congress had previously brought many Federal agencies into the picture with uncertain funding at the local level over time, and the creation of mutually exclusive service networks that have suffered from inadequate staffing. Programs providing long-term funding also required State matching funds and a commitment to a set of services more appropriate for neurotic and psychotic patients than for drug dependent persons. Programs providing short-term financial support have tended to be more generous but generally ended up establishing new treatment institutions apart from established facilities with little promise of funding from any source after the initial 12–15 month grant had run out. Coordination among Federal programs was not required by Congress and was therefore unheard of; evaluation was unknown, although the National Institute of Mental Health (NIMH) was engaged in a national data gathering program that could have become the focus for the evaluation of NIMH-supported facilities. At this writing, the recent designation by Congress and the executive of a single agency with full responsibility for coordinating the overall Federal effort might now lead to the development of an integrated service network at the local level which will be less costly and more effective. Previous efforts by the executive branch to effect coordination through an interagency committee without budgetary authority failed to produce the long-term planning and implementation required to deal with the problem.

In the recent past, Federal funds were available only for "new" program development, whereas an expansion of services in existing structures would have made more sense. By creating many "new" programs in the community, Federally supported projects inadvertently demoralized established programs and contributed to a game of "musical chairs" at the local level. In this game, the same professionals moved around among multiple programs, drawn by the higher salaries and "greater challenge" of the new facility, but resulting in chaos and confusion at the service end. Addicted patients require long-term investment by facilities staffed by nonitinerant professionals and nonprofessionals. Moreover, the emphasis on support of "new" services in existing legislation often led to deceit, and an undue emphasis on novelty and fads in grant applications. Finally, most of the explicit Federal support for the development of service programs has been aimed at the treatment of the heroin addict. This unnecessarily limits the focus to one type of drug and inadvertently creates conditions for dishonesty among service programs whose staffs feel a legitimate need to develop services for all drug dependent states.

EVOLUTION OF FEDERAL SUPPORT

The following describes the evolution of the Federal support program to date. The history is important in understanding the motivation behind the unprecedented executive reorganization authorized by President Nixon.

In 1966, Congress passed the Narcotic Rehabilitation Act which empowered the Surgeon General to set up two distinct (and different) health care systems for addicted patients. On the one hand, it created a civil commitment program administered by the Surgeon General and a prisoner program administered by the Bureau of Prisons, while, on the other hand, it provided more limited financial support for a community-based approach. The latter was set up under the rather generous conditions of matching 90 percent Federal support to 10 percent State support in the initial granting year for staffing, operations, and maintenance costs. The Federal contribution was to decline over five years with the state committed to maintain the total effort at the end of that period. This legislation empowered the executive to develop the program over a two-year period. The delays in clearance through the Bureau of the Budget and the Department of Health, Education and Welfare were cleared away approximately six months before the allocation was to run out and the National Institute of Mental Health staff hurriedly prepared regulations, guidelines, and applications and sent staff around the country in order to locate potential programs. Six programs were selected at a total cost of approximately four million dollars. When the original allocation ran out in July 1968, Congress eliminated the generous terms of the 1966 legislation and limited Federal support to 75 percent of staffing costs only, requiring the States to provide 25 percent of personnel costs and the total burden for operations and main-tenance. Moreover, this "new" program required the States to locate addiction treatment facilities within community mental health centers. The Federal regulations required the establish-ment of five "essential services" [1] for addicts, although it was not clear that all such services would be "essential" in treating opiate dependence. This came at a time when State legislatures were already reluctant to continue their involvement with com-munity mental health center funding which had committed them to match Federal funds at an increasing rate over a five-year period. The change in the conditions of Federal support of drug treatment services jeopardized an expansion of facilities at a time when heroin usage was beginning to spread into suburban areas and among pre-adolescent youth in the inner cities.

Two years later, when funds for this program came up again for renewal, President Nixon announced that he was agreeing to the continued expansion "with great reluctance," thus casting a pall upon the program and its future. The Presi-dent's statement raised additional questions at the State and local levels about the wisdom of matching State funds to a Federal program with an uncertain future. Thus, in four years the guidelines for Federal funding in one specific program have undergone very significant changes. Confusion in drawing pro-gram directions by Congress and the Executive has generally been further compounded by a failure to enlarge significantly the quality and numbers of Federal agency staff charged with committing funds. The result at the local level is considerable "noise" and confusion because of shifting guidelines and in-adequate consultation.

In contrast to other Federal agencies given funds for drug addiction treatment, the National Institute of Mental Health's support program for community-based services seems like a model of reason and order. In 1966, Congress gave 12

---

[1] The five essential services included inpatient, outpatient, partial hospitalization, emergency, and consultation. While these services form the core of community mental health services, they were not specifically designed for addict-related programs.

million dollars to the Office of Economic Opportunity to set up local drug addiction treatment programs. Funds were appropriated in the early spring of 1967, and OEO had to spend this money before July 1, 1967. OEO lacked any expertise in this area and did not even have a knowledgeable group of advisers on problems of the addicted. In contrast to the NIMH funding which was on a matching basis for a period of approximately five years, OEO provided 100 percent support for one year of operation with no assurance that any funds would be available in the second year. Given the huge problems of staffing a program in the first year of operation, this kind of financial support made absolutely no sense. With the urgency required by OEO for the completion of applications, and the uncertainty of future support, experienced programs generally avoided the source of Federal money. In general, the thrust of the OEO effort was to place drug treatment programs in neighborhood health centers. The neighborhood health program directors were naive about addiction but desperate for funds to continue their medical care operations. In many ways these local people felt obliged to jump into new areas while lacking any clear sense of direction. The immediate, short-term wealth of the inexperienced contrasted with the relative poverty of established programs that were ineligible for Federal funds despite their greater expertise in the field of addiction.

Since 1967, the situation has become even more complicated. The Department of Housing and Urban Development got into the act through projected family life centers in model neighborhoods. The family life centers which make some sense in the context of the community organization needs of impoverished ghetto areas are generally functioning as unconnected islands of service quite separate from established health and mental health facilities. They are inappropriate locations for drug addiction treatment. Moreover, funding of these programs is generally on a year to year basis with the expectation that some local or State sources should assume full responsibility after the first year of operation. Given the dearth of local and State funds for established health and welfare services, this idea has been little more than a pipe dream (perhaps an appropriate metaphor when speaking of addiction).

More recently, the Department of Justice was empowered to fund drug treatment facilities under the Safe Streets Act. Funding is reviewed on a regional basis, but is limited to a 12-month period. The expectation seems to be that what is set in motion by the Federal government will logically be continued with local money. Where Federal funding has gone to "new" facilities unconnected to established State, private, or municipal agencies, this is an unlikely outcome. Yet coordination of effort at any level of government (and certainly between Federal and local agencies) has been rare.

Finally, at this writing, the Veteran's Administration and the Department of Defense are being urged to develop services for returning veterans. It is hoped that here the Congress and Executive will appreciate the importance of assuming total responsibility for the care of these unfortunate people by committing significant funds to establish and maintain long-term, inpatient, outpatient, and partial hospitalization services. The care of persons addicted to heroin in Vietnam should not fall to the States; it is clearly a Federal responsibility.

The problems of developing a coherent national policy on drug addiction treatment are mirrored as well in the problems of developing a coherent approach to education. Here, three agencies[2] have been involved with widely different philosophies and expertise. The educational messages of the Department of Justice and the National Institute of Mental Health have differed in emphasis and content leading to a certain amount of "noise" in the message conveyed to the young. The materials produced by NIMH have generally been excellent and well received by young and informed audiences. The information disseminated by the Department of Justice has been tainted all too often with the discredited approaches of the Federal Bureau of Narcotics. The mixture of messages from

[2] The three agencies are the Office of Education, the Department of Justice, and NIMH. The separate services in the Department of Defense have also been similarly divorced from each other in approaching the prevention of drug abuse.

three agencies is not consistent with a public health approach.

The difficulty of the Federal government in coping with the present epidemic is more evidence of the problems associated with all efforts to solve social problems on a large scale during the past decade. Congress launches "new" programs with a flourish, but frequently fails to provide funds to develop and sustain them at the local level. It also fails, at the same time, to staff the necessary bureaucratic support structure within Federal agencies. Thus, visible efforts (as reported in the press) often do not reflect the commitment of the Federal government to the solution of a problem. It appears that only in the creation of superagencies, with significant long-term support, have the Executive branch and the Congress demonstrated a commitment toward goal achievement. One often asks whether NASA could have put a man on the moon with the same obstacles faced by a number of Federal agencies in drug addiction program development. Despite these obstacles, a number of NIMH-supported community-based programs have gotten off the ground and are functioning in a creative manner. As of March 31, 1971, nearly 7,500 patients were receiving care in these facilities. An additional 2,100 patients were being treated in the Federal civil commitment program.

Obviously, there is a need for a greater effort in this area. There have been various proposals for a restructuring of functions at the Federal level. Some have proposed the establishment of a super-agency, analogous to NASA, which would be responsible for all aspects of the Federal drug abuse program. In some other countries the enforcement and health roles are linked in a single administrative structure as a means of effecting coordination. Even in this country, the Federal Bureau of Narcotics and the Public Health Service (responsible for drug addiction treatment) were once both lodged in the Treasury Department. Recently, several academic psychiatrists urged that all aspects of the Federal effort be located in a single agency within HEW (in testimony before Congress). This would theoretically emphasize the public health implications of the enforcement, education, and treatment responsibilities as defined in Washington.

Alternatively, some mental health professionals have suggested the funding of all community-based treatment facilities through NIMH. Funds from OEO, HUD, and the Department of Justice (which had been previously allocated for competing service facilities) would be transferred to NIMH whose guidelines for funding would be made more flexible. Smaller grants could be made available for partial services in the initial years of program operation rather than the present mechanism which requires the simultaneous establishment of five services in the first year of operation. The costs of the first year of staffing, operations, and maintenance are usually less than in subsequent years because of the difficulties inherent in staffing and launching new programs. A greater percentage of Federal support for staffing, operations, and maintenance could then be made available over a ten-year period so that services could develop rationally in response to need and the effectiveness of operations. Long-term Federal support set up in this manner theoretically would encourage partnership with States and municipalities. Finally, this funding structure would have to allow agencies that are not community mental health centers to apply for funds. The appropriate local recipient should be defined at the State or municipal level and permit linkages with previously unaffiliated therapeutic communities. Participation in a nation-wide evaluation program would be a condition of funding. The development of educational materials would be within HEW in the Office of Education or NIMH. The previous multiplicity of messages emanating from the several involved agencies would have to come to an end. In the absence of an all-embracing super-agency, enforcement would remain with the Department of Justice.

THE WHITE HOUSE INITIATIVE

In June 1971, the President moved dramatically to reorganize rehabilitation, research, and prevention efforts in the civilian area while utilizing the expertise of a number of consultants to improve the quality of care to drug dependent men in the military. In an unusual Executive reorganization, the

President proposed the creation of a special office in the White House, responsible to him, and having control over the portions of the budgets of civilian agencies which deal with drug abuse treatment, prevention, and research. This Special Action Office on Drug Abuse Prevention would thus control portions of the budgets of agencies within HEW (including the National Institute of Mental Health and the Office of Education), OEO, Department of Labor, Department of Transportation, Department of Housing and Urban Development, Veteran's Administration, and the Bureau of Prisons. Through consultation to the Department of Defense, this office would also improve treatment and prevention services in the military. The Department of Justice was not included in the reorganization, thus continuing the separation of health and enforcement responsibility. Nevertheless, the early stages of reorganization were marked by a degree of cooperation from individuals within the Bureau of Narcotics and Dangerous Drugs that differed from previously established patterns of interaction with health agencies. While the President was criticized for further politicizing the drug abuse problem by locating the office in the White House, he selected a non-political, highly competent professional to head the program. As described elsewhere in this chapter (and book), Dr. Jerome Jaffe had previously demonstrated unique qualities of scientific expertise and management ability in developing the Illinois State Drug House Program in that State's Department of Mental Health. He had worked under both Democratic and Republican governors and had concentrated his efforts toward making treatment widely available, on a voluntary basis, with an elaborate evaluation program tied into the treatment effort.

Dr. Jaffe's early efforts in Washington have been focused on the heroin problem. He has moved to establish a national data bank with a unique identification system that assures confidentiality and an accurate "count." Future support of community-based services will be tied to a management approach whereby funding is geared to performance and performance is assessed on the basis of patient data (numbers of patients and quality of care). A multimodality system (analogous to Illinois) will be encouraged at the local level. There will be an expansion of training for all care-givers on a regional and a national basis with a National Training Center located in the Washington-Baltimore area and regional training upgraded and made more relevant. Areas of research are to be targeted for special emphasis including epidemiologic studies (follow-up of Vietnam veterans), research and development of a long-acting narcotic antagonist and long-acting opiate substitutes, clinical evaluation, and studies of health care delivery.

The Special Action Office is a unique creation which may preserve existing organizational lines while improving functional capability. While some have criticized the location of the office at the White House, this has improved communication of individual agency needs to the highest levels of the Federal government. The staffing requirements and funding regulations can be realistically applied in the Office of Management and Budget, with Jaffe's staff in communication with all interested parties and defining priorities among agencies. If the reorganization works, it will be an extraordinary accomplishment.

The obstacles to the program are formidable. Interagency squabbling will now focus on Jaffe and his new operation. There will be resentment in the agencies about his role in directing "their" policies and they will likely seek to withhold information in order to preserve their "turf." In the end, they may appreciate that his position can improve their own roles, but it will take considerable understanding on all sides.

The Congress has yet to act on the new reorganization. The final form of the new office (which is to have a time limit of three years plus an optional two years) has yet to be decided. At this writing, however, it is clear that some reorganization of the Federal program has been necessary in order to provide a single knowledgeable position (backed up by expert consultation) and a coordinated set of services to the local level. This will likely not "solve" the drug problem, but it may make it more manageable and our response more appropriate.

THE STATE LEVEL: LOBBYING AND NEGOTIATING

At the State level, treatment services have generally been funded out of existing Departments of Mental Health, Public Health, or new agencies chartered with the task of developing drug addiction service facilities.[3] In at least two States, competing City and State drug treatment programs espousing different philosophies, have led to considerable confusion. The most extraordinary example of this is the competing New York State and New York City systems that were separately developed in 1966. New York City opted for an ideologically narrow approach under Dr. Ramirez (see Chapter 4) while New York State developed an expensive civil commitment program, while also managing to support more limited programs of methadone maintenance and one joint State-City run therapeutic community.

Massachusetts has a State-run program which espouses a self-help approach, funding 60 separate voluntary programs at a total cost of $1 million in the first year of operation. The City of Boston utilizes methadone maintenance treatment almost exclusively, but its lightly staffed program is limited by inadequate funding at the City level and lack of interest at the State level. In both New York and Massachusetts, there is, in general, a failure to coördinate the treatment systems so that individuals failing in one modality might be efficiently picked up elsewhere. The State system which has worked best is in the State of Illinois. Here a single individual (Dr. Jerome Jaffe) had responsibility for developing drug treatment programs throughout the State. He developed a coordinated network of services, some operated directly and some under State contract. The State provided evaluation as well as urine testing

[3] Educational programs for school children of different ages have been coördinated by the appropriate State Department of Education while enforcement functions reside in special police units. Most of the enforcement role at the local level falls to local police forces rather than Federal agents.

and required any State-funded program to provide urines for screening as well as other data on patients admitted to treatment. No State was as fortunate as Illinois to have someone of Dr. Jaffe's brilliance and leadership to limit the propagation of poorly controlled programs while directing the establishment of well-run State-operated facilities.

It is obvious that at the level of administration, as well as of program operation, power is an important factor in effecting program implementation. Generally, there has been a leadership vacuum at the Federal level and within most State and municipal agencies chartered with responsibility in this area. While some problems can be blamed on funding difficulty, there has been too much uncertainty in situations demanding decisiveness and too much ideology in situations demanding flexibility. The control of methadone distribution is one example where decisive leadership could eliminate diversion. In other areas, ideological commitment to a single therapeutic approach has led to situations where many patients receive no treatment at all.

Jaffe's work in Illinois, DuPont's work in Washington, D.C., and the work of a few other individuals around the country are impressive because they accepted the mantle of power to implement programs despite obstacles from community groups and local bureaucracy. To support their programs, these leaders have turned repeatedly to legislators who have generally been responsive to a clearly directed message about reasonable program goals and objectives. Obviously, any new program must compete with other priorities on the legislative agenda, but because of national and local concern about drug abuse, legislators have generally been responsive to these service needs. Where a program director has already obtained a Federal grant from NIMH or another Federal agency, legislators are generally more responsive to giving funds for program development. Obviously, written support by responsible State and local agencies (as well as significant community groups) is important in the lobbying effort.

Few health care professionals are skilled in the art of lobbying. Consultation is usually of great value in identifying and soliciting the support of key legislative leaders who can influence the course of the State or municipal budget through a Committee on Ways and Means (or its equivalent). Adequate information is the name of the game. Items can be removed or added at a moment's notice in the Committee meeting and once the budget is passed, it is too late to make changes. Any program requiring local government funds would do well to solicit the support of powerful legislators as well as urban affairs and health advisors to the governor and/or mayor.

Lobbying and negotiating must go on after the legislature has acted on the budget. Budgetary changes can be made within the Executive branch that could seriously cripple a program. In contrast to Federal bureaucrats, officials in some States are encouraged to return funds at the end of each fiscal year rather than spend every cent appropriated. This means that budgets are written in such a way that some staff positions could never be filled and some items never purchased. Most States require line item budgets prepared two years in advance by the program director. When it comes time to purchase an item, it is no longer needed while another previously unsolicited piece of equipment is urgently required. This is the kind of situation that exhausts program directors committed to treatment goals but dealing with middle level civil servants who are in no hurry to respond to requests from higher paid professionals. Moreover, the bureaucrat in this case recognizes that the State budget requires the non-expenditure of funds and can usually disallow the request on some minor technical point. If the program director is bound to the line item budget, he must consider the priority of his request since it will be emotionally impossible for him to develop an appeal case for every piece of equipment. Appeals are possible, however, and here again alliances with powerful elected officials are the key to moving the bureaucracy.

In some States, civil service regulations make program implementation an impossibility. Many drug treatment programs are now employing ex-addicts in administrative and counseling roles and most ex-addicts have criminal records that bar them from State employment. In general, civil service structures are inflexible and tend to inhibit program development by restrictions on hiring, salaries, and civil service examination. These procedures usually end up excluding the ex-addict counselor with a criminal record and without a high school diploma. Some States (e.g., Connecticut) have set up within the civil service structure new categories of mental health care allowing personnel whose qualifications are readily met by ex-addict graduates of established treatment programs. These civil service categories include sufficient flexibility so that individuals may move up into positions of responsibility appropriate to their talents. Other States would benefit from the experiences in Connecticut.

The emotional importance to established civil servants of any challenge to the status quo cannot be underestimated. Ex-addicts making $7,000 to $10,000 a year are considered threats by established civil servants who make no more themselves. This is an extremely tense issue with moral justification on both sides; but the reality is that programs can be impeded if not vigorously supported by elected officials to whom middle-level State civil servants report.

Line item budget restrictions, resistance of local bureaucrats, and the problems of the State civil service system are a nightmare for any program director. It is imperative that he have control of his own budget to meet the unforeseen events that inevitably plague drug addiction treatment programs. In most places, however, this is rare. It can be done through a "contract for services" mechanism between the State or municipal agency and the treatment program. Such contracts are also consistent with the terms of most Federal granting programs. The State agency agrees to pay a fixed annual sum to the treatment facility for services rendered to addicts. Terms of the contract may or may not permit the treatment agency to collect private fees or medicaid. This mechanism, which should be negotiated with lawyers for both parties, gives the program director moment to moment options to operate within a fixed amount of money. Personnel may be paid without regard to civil service regulations and necessary equipment may be purchased. The

State may require monthly vouchers for funds spent during the preceding month.

In general, it takes considerable effort to work out the administrative structures which can reasonably support a local drug treatment facility. At different times, it may involve discreet confrontation with State officials and the assistance of sympathetic journalists who can wield considerable influence through the media in helping programs get started. If a program lacks political muscle somewhere in the administrative structure, or through available consultation, it will likely flounder at some point. It is important to have someone on staff (or in a consultative capacity) who understands and can assist the manipulation of events by keeping an eye on the course of procedures within the State structure that might otherwise inhibit local program development. In my experience, the lobbying and information gathering at the State level is infinitely more difficult than obtaining a Federal grant from any of the Federal agencies.

THE COMMUNITY LEVEL: PROBLEMS AND PERILS

The situation at the local community level is even more complex, especially when one is dealing with the problem of heroin addiction in a minority group population. To the liberal professional living in the suburbs, the words "community control" and "power to the people" strike a very sympathetic chord. Black people, after all, have been enslaved and have not really achieved their measure of freedom until recently. Well-meaning and sympathetic whites coming into this situation inevitably get burned and hurt by the complexity of political forces within the community. In communities with an unemployment rate approaching 25 percent, community control usually means the employment of indigenous personnel. Where a certain number of indigenous personnel are *trained* for meaningful jobs, this can be a real asset to a developing program. Where these persons are not trained and where program directors have no control of hiring and firing practices, community control is an unmitigated disaster. There are few health programs that began with the burden of community control and continue to survive. Real control means monetary control; and ultimate budgetary decisions are made at the State or Federal level. Even with "contract for services" budgeting, the annual appropriation is made by the State and vouchers are received monthly by State civil servants. Thus, false expectations are set up within the community and their rage is focused upon the program people who are more visible than State or Federal bureaucrats when expectations cannot be met.

In practice, community control means control by a politically sophisticated group within the local area and not control by the consumer population. In addiction, this may mean that the local community is hostile to the addict and demands vigilante-type activity in response to the addiction problem. This point of view can be advocated by politically sophisticated area leaders on the right side of the political spectrum. On the left are those who view addicts as the revolutionary vanguard. Successful treatment is perceived as a threat to the revolution. Additionally, sympathetic whites are seen as a threat to the ideology that identifies the white man in totally negative terms. As seen from the vantage point of four hundred years of history, this may have a functional component. When viewed in the present, with the opportunity to begin to cope with heroin addiction, it destroys a program more effectively than anything ever dreamed up in State or Federal regulations.

It is my feeling that a drug addiction treatment program in a facility with a strong degree of community control cannot be run by a white psychiatrist with any degree of success because of the tremendous pressures being placed upon him and the accusations of racism that impede his every move. In most situations he is "dammed if he does and damned if he doesn't." However, even a black director will not be immune to the extraordinary pressures generated by community power groups. In this situation it is very difficult to act upon clinical judgment. In some locations it was felt that the selection of some more militant person from the community as director (or in some other responsible position) would cool things sufficiently to allow clinical judgment to prevail. On the contrary, this has destroyed programs; the black racism of the militant individual causes him to attack the clinical posture of the physicians and staff as "elitist" or "racist." Programs so afflicted are best left to die.

Community-based treatment services which have gotten off the ground have negotiated with community leaders to set up services in an area, but have not given in to the demand for "community control" or "sharing of power" in day to day operations. There is an accountability to community in terms of the quality of health care given. It is easier to launch this type of program from the State or city level; it is much more difficult to launch such a program when it serves primarily the needs of a single politically conscious community.

It is obvious that the skills that it takes to write and to develop a proposal for a Federal grant may be different from the skills that it takes to successfully manipulate State and city government to effect implementation of a program. Moreover, these skills in turn are quite different from the techniques involved in keeping a program afloat in the midst of extraordinary pressures from the community. In the field of addiction, these go beyond the questions of community control. Some program directors have allegedly received threats of violence from persons involved in drug sale and distribution, particularly when these program leaders were instituting large-scale methadone maintenance programs. On the other side, the police often view with considerable ambivalence the development of drug treatment programs. While it is impossible to provide liaison to the drug distributors in hopes of quieting their activity, it is desirable to establish an active liaison with local police forces. In the beginning, some police officials will regard a new treatment facility as a "source" of information. The patients will be suspicious of this role as well. It is, therefore, imperative that the police be politely informed on the need for confidentiality of all information obtained by clinic staff. Rather, the statements by police officials that the thrust of their efforts is aimed at distributors and dealers rather than individual "junkies" should be supported by efforts to help them to get the patient into treatment (on short notice) as an alternative to incarceration.

Most police forces welcome this development. Moreover, consultation to law enforcement agencies should include in-service education of police officers on the pharmacology, psychology, and culture of drug usage as well as direct assistance to them in their efforts to prevent drug abuse by lectures and films. The police are quite aware that scare tactics developed in previous years usually fall on deaf ears among the present generation of students. They are aware that their image has been hurt by the ongoing civil war between police forces and the National Guard on the one hand, and students and minority group radicals on the other. Police want sympathetic understanding from mental health professionals and some help in improving their image and effectiveness. The staff of a new drug treatment program can provide in-service education to police officers on the problems associated with specific drugs and can help to correct false stereotypes and myths which inhibit the policeman's effectiveness both as a law enforcement person as well as in his role as community educator. It is important that the local treatment facility impress the local narcotics control unit with efforts to limit diversion of drugs, particularly methadone, so that the law enforcement authorities will understand that the treatment facility is not the source of illicit drugs and is providing a full range of rehabilitation services designed to treat the total scope of the problem.

In addition to the police, consultation should be made available to the schools, medical service facilities, and multiservice centers in the area served by the drug addiction treatment facility. These agencies are often inhibited in their work by ignorance and misinformation about drugs and drug abuse. Effective consultation makes them more effective in their work while cementing important political linkages for the drug treatment facility.

In summary, the development of a comprehensive range of services for drug dependent patients at the community level involves a series of negotiations with several different levels of government, each demanding different tactics and techniques in order to negotiate an effective program. Any local facility which sets out to deal with the problems of heroin addiction and psychological, adverse reactions of hallucinogenic drug abuse requires an infusion of funds. The largest source of such funds is the Federal government,[4] but different Federal agencies have different funding requirements. In many ways, the National Institute of Mental Health, which provides funds to community mental health centers, is the most realistic Federal support structure because it commits the Federal government to long-term funding (albeit on a matching fund basis). NIMH support, however, is for staffing costs only and requires an infusion of State or local funds for operations and maintenance. The restrictions on funding to mental health centers or affiliates of such facilities prevents the funding of some promising programs. OEO, the Department of Justice, and H.U.D. are alternative funding sources, but short-term support (12 months–15 months) places severe limitations on long-term programming. Applications to any particular Federal agency should consider the preferred priorities of that agency's funding effort. Unaffiliated treatment programs would do well to affiliate with agencies that are eligible for Federal funding.

As a general rule, Federal agencies have tended to respond favorably to program applications consisting of a consortium of service institutions under the imprimatur of a city or State agency having responsibility for drug addiction treatment. Grant applications should reflect knowledge of the different treatment modalities as well as the social and demographic characteristics of the area served. Crime and welfare rates, and drug-related death and arrest rates should be described in order to justify the need for services as well as to provide a baseline of data against which one can later assess the impact of the new intervention. The location and description of existing services should be provided as well as some explanation of the relationship of proposed programs to gaps in the existing network. The grant application should include positions for health professionals (M.D.'s, nurses, psychologists, social workers, etc.) and ex-addicts in a variety of positions.

---

[4] A number of therapeutic communities have relied exclusively on voluntary contributions. This is a distinct art with which the author has not had personal experience.

Some provision for in-service training should be spelled out; it may refer these needs to an established affiliated service program. Data collection and analysis capability are desirable to document, as is support by relevant local and official organizations. Staffing patterns should reflect a seven-day–week facility. There should be some assurance from relevant agencies that adequate space will be available for program development. Finally, the application should request funds for the development of all treatment modalities for the heroin addict with the capacity based on estimates of need. This "multimodality approach" is essentially a conglomerate of approaches proposed in Chapters 2, 3, 4, and 6.

Below the Federal level, the principal issue in program development involves the negotiation of sufficient power to be free to make decisions based upon clinical realities. This means the freedom to budget flexibly according to acute and emergent needs as well as for the long-term. It also means the ability to hire staff who might otherwise be ineligible for hiring under State civil service regulations. Thus, in negotiations at the State level, one should seek sufficient power in order that a program's goals are not blocked. Apart from the budgetary and civil service restrictions, some States also require the submission of data to the Department of Public Health for later forwarding to enforcement agencies. This restriction upon program independence discourages patients from seeking treatment and, alternatively, encourages them to lie about their names and other identifiable data. Obviously, the freedom to withhold this information is important for the program director.

The issue of power is equally important at the community level. Competing power groups within the community demand to control programs for goals that frequently run counter to the interests of addiction treatment. No facility should voluntarily accept community control and those that are hassled with it will have to find some way of mitigating its objectionable effects. What is required is a system of community accountability which informs and advises the community about addiction treatment and its implications. At various times it falls upon the treatment agency to adopt Machiavellian tactics to utilize community forces in negotiating more power from the State and to utilize State forces in restricting the demands of the community politicians. This is an extremely difficult task and one can play the game only infrequently because miscalculations are inevitable.

One cannot underestimate the importance of discreet confrontations[5] as well as the importance of power in the establishment and maintenance of drug treatment programs. The most effective program directors have been those who have established a power base from the State and not yielded it to community politicians. If it is possible to effect alliances with individual power groups within the community, this is an important plus. One such power group is the police and it is important to provide liaison to them. Other power groups may be multi-service centers and other agencies whose work is frequently impeded by addicts in families or addicts who are being served in other ways. The provision of service to these troublesome patients in a partnership arrangement frequently leads to effective linkages in the community. It is the development of these linkages (plus continued funding from State and/or Federal sources) that assures program continuity.

After these various complicated negotiations, it almost seems incredible that one could have the energy left to deal with the troublesome patients and often difficult staff that work for a drug treatment program. Ex-addicts can be as demanding as the patient population. The relationships between ex-addicts, social workers, nurses, and psychiatrists can be extremely complicated in the situation where the ex-addict is demanding to be a full member of the treatment team on a par with the other professionals in all respects, including pay. This presents problems, particularly for nurses and social workers who are not paid as much as physicians and who may resent those ex-addicts who are being paid more than they. However, in a drug addic-

[5] Threatened mass staff resignations and shutdowns are commonly employed threats in this regard. The fear of such reports reaching the press can often move bureaucratic obstacles. In every confrontation, however, a program loses equity which limits effectiveness if confrontations must repeatedly occur.

tion treatment program, it is the quality of contribution of the individual rather than his professional degree which should determine his salary and his responsibilities. In the beginning, and throughout the history of local programs, this kind of conflict will be inevitable. It will occasionally result in losing valuable professionals who are not able to work in this kind of situation. The ex-addict per se is not a treatment agent merely because he has stopped using drugs. Rather, it is the skill of the individual and his own experience which should determine his value to the program. Trained ex-addict counselors, experienced in group therapy, will often be valued by professionals in an interdisciplinary team treatment unit.

Program staff often find it important to engage in group process interactions in order to deal with the conflicts and tensions between individuals and disciplines and as a result of dealing with this very troublesome patient population. Different programs will choose different ways of coping with internal staff conflicts. What is clear is that the staff tends to move from crisis to crisis, and that it takes a strong and sensitive director to facilitate the resolution of these crises so that team personnel may move on to cope with the treatment problems presented by the patients and the maintenance of the program. Such conflicts arise in methadone maintenance treatment programs, detoxification programs, free clinics, and therapeutic communities.

It is clear that the implementation and maintenance of a treatment program for drug dependent persons requires a great deal of effort with daily and unrelenting pressures that could undermine program effectiveness. It is always important, therefore, to define program goals so that these may be measured and effectiveness assessed. Goals may be defined temporally in terms of the bench marks to be obtained after one, two, and three years of operation. They may be also defined in terms of programs in primary, secondary, and tertiary prevention as these have been described in the Introduction; and the specific approaches to tertiary prevention or rehabilitation described in other chapters.

There is now in existence no perfect program to deal with the epidemic of drug dependence in the United States.

This epidemic can only become worse with the expected influx of Vietnam War veterans addicted to heroin. Nevertheless, a number of approaches to rehabilitation, particularly of heroin addiction, have been defined and these are available to interested communities. For the most part, communities where no services exist require the development of a new network of services for the heroin addict. The problem of heroin addiction is better understood than the other drug dependencies and the range of services which have developed is also better understood than the range of needs associated with the other drug dependencies. Moreover, the problem of heroin addiction is most visible in lower class communities because of crime and the damage to the afflicted individual who is likely to die before age 35.

It has been found that no single treatment program is appropriate for all heroin addicts, and that all programs require some degree of motivation. For the most part, methadone maintenance treatment requires the least motivation, but ancillary services are clearly indicated in order that the patient not use the facility as a mere "connection." Methadone maintenance treatment is perhaps the simplest to establish in terms of cost, and the use of traditional facilities, but involves risks in terms of diversion and the addiction of unaddicted persons. These risks can be minimized in seven-day–week services which do not allow methadone to leave the clinic unless a patient has proven himself responsible through a prolonged period of treatment. No patient should be forced into a maintenance treatment program. Viable therapeutic communities and detoxification facilities plus outpatient group therapy must be available as alternative service modalities. Finally, innovative programs are clearly indicated for the adolescent patient because the most popular modes of treatment (including civil commitment, methadone maintenance, and therapeutic communities) are not appropriate for this patient group. Behavioral modification, narcotic-blocking drugs, educational programs, and group psychotherapy all might be applied in different degrees.

The use of hallucinogens and marihuana involves a certain risk of acute adverse reactions and a poorly defined risk of chronic sequelae, including amotivational syndromes, psychoses, chronic anxiety, and/or depressive disorders. We are only dimly able to perceive the relative role of these drugs in the etiology of the behavioral problems presented by adolescents today, because of the massive social changes that have occurred in this country and in the Western World in the last ten years. Nevertheless, drug usage is certainly a part of the syndrome and may be involved in the unfortunate end stages of dropping out which have been observed and described in Chapter 6. Free clinics administering to the acute adverse reactions and medical problems of itinerant youth are an important service in a truly comprehensive program. The need for continuity of care requires that these free clinics be affiliated with established mental health facilities which would provide long-term psychiatric treatment to enable patients to integrate the powerful experiences of the hallucinogenic drug state. Such alliances may not be easy to effect. Where, however, volunteer free clinic staff are affiliated at some point in their work day with more formal institutions they should encourage the development of such referrals. Alternatively, free clinics have welcomed mental health consultants to come in, provided that these consultants respect the life style and demeanor of the patients and do not confront head-on the "movement" aspect of the life style. Given this constraint, it is quite possible for mental health professionals to relate to the individual problems of adaptation presented by these young people.

Treating barbiturate and hypnotic-sedative dependence is a complicated individual problem of medical care management which may be carried out in a hospital setting or in a special regional detoxification facility. The problems of amphetamine overdose and withdrawal also require some sort of inpatient intervention. Overdose from amphetamines can be treated in a straightforward manner as described in Chapter 5, but withdrawal requires attention to a painful psychological depression which, if untreated, leads to relapsing drug-using behavior. The stickler in treating these forms of drug abuse is the problem of chronic relapsing behavior which is not well-understood and for which there are no established treatment modalities. Until such time as we have a clearer idea of what works, it would seem that a variety of approaches can and should be attempted.

It is impossible even in the space of some two hundred pages to communicate the complexity of a problem and the prospects for approaching its solution. In the recent past neither in the Federal government nor in the vast majority of States have we begun to grapple with the administrative issues that would make community-based treatment a reality. If the visible response of the press to the epidemic has been a measure of our concern, the manifest response of the different levels of government in terms of visible and viable treatment programs is some measure of the community's helplessness to meet this massive epidemic. There are no ready solutions, but the partial solutions offer some hope for some control of the problem in the individual and the prospect of moving at the community level toward a more rational approach to a solution. New Haven, Connecticut, Chicago, Illinois, Washington, D.C., and a few other locations have made a start toward the community-wide control of the problem of heroin addiction. It would seem appropriate at this time to begin to incorporate the various technologies that have evolved over the last ten years into rational programs throughout the country based upon these approaches.

Comprehensive programming in any community cannot emerge in one step. It must evolve gradually wherein individual components are developed in response to a specific need. Eventually, a core of integrated services should evolve which are consistently evaluated in terms of their effectiveness and the need for modifications. A commitment by the Federal government for long-term support and a commitment at the State level to assure implementation will go a long way toward removing drug abuse from the political arena and placing it in the public health sphere where appropriate solutions are possible.

Given the history of the Federal effort in this area and the obstacles which exist at the community and State level, a book like this cannot have a "happy ending" nor propose optimism for the future. It is perhaps ironic that the drug abuse epidemic of the past decade has been symptomatic of the massive social changes going on in this country, Western Europe, and Japan. Our failure to develop adequate institutions to meet the drug problem has been consistent with our failures in all of the social programs during this time. There have, however, been some bright spots and it is these successful local examples which suggest that some progress is possible.

Bibliography

Introduction

Blum, R. H., *et al.*, *Horatio Alger's Children: Observations on Student Drug Use* (San Francisco: Jossey-Bass, 1968).

Brotman, R., Meyer, A. S., and Freedman, A. M., An approach to treating narcotic addicts based on a community mental health diagnosis, "Comprehensive Psychiatry," 6:104–118, 1965.

Caplan, G., *Principles of Preventive Psychiatry* (New York: Basic Books, 1964).

Cheek, F., Exploratory study of drugs and social interaction, "Archives of General Psychiatry," 9:566, 1963.

Chein, I., Gerald, D. L., Lee, R. S., and Rosenfeld, E., *The Road to H* (New York: Basic Books, 1964).

Clausen, J. A., Drug Addiction, in R. K. Merton and R. A. Nisbet (eds.), *Contemporary Social Problems* (New York: Harcourt Brace, 1961), pp. 181–221.

Clausen, J. A., Social patterns, personality and adolescent drug use, in A. H. Leighton, J. A. Clausen, and R. Wilson (eds.), *Explorations in Social Psychiatry* (New York: Basic Books, 1957), pp. 230–277.

Duvall, H. J., Locke, B. Z., and Brill, L., Follow-up study of narcotic drug addicts five years after hospitalization, "Public Health Reports," 78:185–193, 1963.

Frosch, W. A., Psychoanalytic evaluation of addiction and habituation, "Journal of American Psychoanalytic Association," 18:209–218, January 1970.

Gerard, D. L., and Kornetsky, C. H., Adolescent opiate addiction: a study of control and addict subjects, "Psychiatric Quarterly," 29:457–486, 1955.

Glover, E. G., On the aetiology of drug-addiction, "International Journal of Psychoanalysis," 13(Part 3):298–328, 1932.

Harms, E., *Drug Addiction and Youth* (New York: Pergamon Press, 1965).

Hill, H., Haertzen, C. A., and Glaser, R., Personality characteristics of narcotic addicts as indicated by the MMPI, "Journal of General Psychology," 62:126–139, 1960.

Jaffe, J. H., Zaks, M. S., and Washington, E. N., Experience with the use of methadone in a multi-modality program for the treatment of narcotics users, "International Journal of Addiction," 4:481–490, 1969.

Mirin, S. M., Shapiro, L. M., Meyer, R. E., Pillard, R. C., and Fisher, S., Casual versus heavy use of marijuana: a redefinition of the marijuana problem, "American Journal of Psychiatry," 127:1134–1140, 1971.

Nowlis, H. H., *Drugs on the College Campus: A Guide for College Administrators* (New York: Doubleday [Anchor], 1969).

O'Donnell, J. A., The relapse rate in narcotic addiction: a critique of follow-up studies in D. M. Wilner and G. G. Kassebaum (eds.), *Narcotics* (New York: McGraw-Hill, 1965).

Robins, L. N., and Murphy, G. E., Drug use in a normal population of young Negro men, "American Journal of Public Health," 57(9):1580–1596, 1967.

Schuster, C. R., and Villarreal, J. E., The experimental analysis of opioid dependence, in D. H. Efron (ed.), *Psychopharmacology: A Review of Progress 1957–1967*, Public Health Service Publication #1836 (Washington, D.C.: U.S. Government Printing Office, 1968), pp. 811–828.

Thompson, T., and Pickens, R., Stimulant self-administration by animals: some comparisons with opiate self-administration, "Federation Proceedings," 29:6–12, January–February 1970.

Wieder, H., and Kaplan, E. H., Drug use in adolescents, "Psychoanalytic Study of the Child," 24:399–431, 1969.

Wikler, A., Conditioning factors in opiate addiction and relapse, in D. M. Wilner and G. G. Kassebaum (eds.), *Narcotics* (New York: McGraw-Hill, 1965).

Winick, C., The drug addict and his treatment, in H. Toch (ed.), *Criminal Psychology* (New York: Holt, Rinehart & Winston, 1961), pp. 357–380.

Chapter 1

Eddy, N. B., Halbach, H., Isbell, H., and Seevers, M. H., Drug dependence: its significance and characteristics, "Bulletin of World Health Organization," 32:721–733, 1965.

Hunt, G. H., and Odoroff, Follow-up study of narcotic addicts after hospitalization, "Public Health Reports," 77:41–54, 1962.

Jaffe, J. H., Drug addiction and drug abuse, in L. S. Goodman and A. Gilman (eds.), *The Pharmacological Basis of Therapeutics*, 3rd edition (New York: Macmillan, 1965), pp. 285–311.

Meyer, R. E., Methods for evaluating drug efficacy in the treatment of drug dependent states, in J. Levine, B. Schiele, and L. Bonthielet (eds.), *Principles and Problems in Establishing Efficacy of Psychotropic Agents*, Public Health Service Publication #2138, Jan 1971, published by American College of Neuropsychopharmacology, U.S. Department of Health, Education, and Welfare, pp. 216–226.

Nelsen, Judith M., Single dose tolerance to morphine sulphate: electroencephalographic correlates in central motivational system (Ph.D. thesis, Boston University Graduate School, 1970).

O'Donnell, J. A., The Relapse rate in narcotic addiction: a critique of follow-up studies, in D. M. Wilner and G. G. Kassebaum (eds.), *Narcotics* (New York: McGraw-Hill, 1965).

Schuster, C. R., and Villarreal, J. E., The experimental analysis of opioid dependence, in D. H. Efron (ed.), *Psychopharmacology: A Review of Progress 1957–1967*, Public Health Service Publication #1836 (Washington, D.C.: U.S. Government Printing Office, 1968), pp. 811–828.

Thompson, T., and Pickens, R., Stimulant self-administration by animals: some comparisons with opiate self-administration, "Federation Proceedings," 29:6–12, January–February 1970.

Wikler, A., Conditioning factors in opiate addiction and relapse, in D. M. Wilner and G. G. Kassebaum (eds.), *Narcotics* (New York: McGraw-Hill, 1965).

Winick, C., The drug addict and his treatment, in H. Toch (ed.), *Criminal Psychology* (New York: Holt, Rinehart & Winston, 1961), pp. 357–380.

Chapter 2

Combined Statement of the Council on Mental Health and Its Committee on Alcoholism and Drug Dependence, American Medical Association, and the Committee on Problems of Drug Dependence, National Research Council, "Methadone maintenance techniques in the management of morphine-type dependence," March 16, 1971.

Dole, V. P., and Nyswander, M. E., Heroin addiction—a metabolic disease, "Archives of Internal Medicine," 120:19–24, 1967.

Dole, V. P., and Nyswander, M. E., A Medical treatment for diacetylmorphine (heroin) addiction, "Journal of American Medical Association," 193(8):646–650, 1965.

Dole, V. P., and Nyswander, M. E., Methadone maintenance and its implications for theories of narcotics addiction, "Research Publications of the Association for Research in Nervous and Mental Disease," 46:359–366, 1968.

Dole, V. P., Nyswander, M. E., and Warner, A., Successful treatment of 750 criminal addicts, "Journal of American Medical Association," 206:2708–2711, 1968.

DuPont, R. L., Heroin addiction treatment and crime reduction (paper presented at American Psychiatric Association, Washington, D.C., May 6, 1971).

Fink, M., and Freedman, A. M., Antagonists in the treatment of opiate dependence, in R. B. Phillipson (ed.), *Modern Trends in Drug Dependence and Alcoholism* (London: Butterworth, 1970), pp. 49–59.

Fink, M., Zaks, A., Sharoff, R., Mora, A., Bruner, A., Leavitt, S., and Freedman, A. M., Naloxone in heroin dependence, "Clinical Pharmacology and Therapeutics," 9:568–577, 1968.

Goldstein, A., Problems of Drug Dependence (report to NAS–NRC Meeting, February 1971, Toronto, Ontario, Canada). The treatment of heroin addiction by methadone maintenance.

Halliday, R., Committee on Problems of Drug Dependence, 28th Meeting, 1966, Appendix 14, p. 4599.

Jaffe, J. H., Comparison of acetylmethadol and methadone in the treatment of long-term heroin users, a pilot study, "Journal of American Medical Association," 211:1834–1839, 1970.

Jaffe, J. H., Psychopharmacology and opiate dependence, in D. H. Efron (ed.), *Psychopharmacology: A Review of Progress 1957–1967,* Public Health Service Publication #1836 (Washington, D.C.: U.S. Government Printing Office, 1968), pp. 853–864.

Jaffe, J. H., Zaks, M. S., and Washington, E. N., Experience with the use of methadone in a multi-modality program for the treatment of narcotics users, "International Journal of Addiction," 4:481–490, 1969.

Martin, W. R., The basis and possible utility of the use of opioid antagonists in the ambulatory treatment of the addict, in A. Wikler (ed.), *The Addictive States* (Baltimore: Williams & Wilkins Co., 1968), p. 367.

Methadone Maintenance Evaluation Committee (the Gearing Committee), Progress report of the evaluation of methadone maintenance treatment program as of March 31, 1968, "Journal of American Medical Association," 206:2712–2714, 1968.

Methadone Maintenance Evaluation Committee of New York, report to the third national conference on methadone treatment in New York, November 4, 1970.

Perkins, M., and Block, H. I., Survey of a methadone maintenance treatment program, "American Journal of Psychiatry," 126(10): 1389–1396, 1970.

Resnick, R., Fink, M., and Freedman, A. M., A cyclazocine typology of opiate dependence, "American Journal of Psychiatry," 126: 1256–1260, 1970.

Wieland, W. F., Methadone maintenance treatment of chronic narcotic addiction, "New Physician," 18:210–211, 1969.

Wieland, W. F., Methadone maintenance treatment of heroin addiction: beginning treatment on an outpatient basis (paper presented at Meeting of American Psychiatric Association, Boston, Mass., May 17, 1968).

Wikler, A., Interaction of physical dependence on classical and operant conditioning on the genesis of relapse, in A. Wikler (ed.), *The Addictive States* (Baltimore: Williams & Wilkins Co., 1968), pp. 280–287.

Zaks, A., Jones, T., Fink, M., and Freedman, A. M., Naloxone treatment of opiate dependence, a progress report, "Journal of American Medical Association," 215:2108–2110, 1971.

Chapter 3

Bewley, T. H., Heroin addiction in the United Kingdom (1959–1964), "British Journal of Medicine," 5473:1284–1286, 1965.

Brain, R., The report of the interdepartmental committee on drug addiction, "British Journal of Addictions," 57:81–103, 1961.

Diskind, M., Meyer, H., and Klonsky, G., A second look at the New York State parole drug experiment, "Federal Probation," 24(4):34–41, December 1964.

Jones, M., *The Therapeutic Community: New Treatment Method in New York* (New York: Basic Books, 1953).

Kramer, J. C., The state vs. the addict: uncivil commitment, "Boston University Law Review," 50(1):1–22, Winter 1970.

Kramer, J. C., and Bass, R. A., Institutionalized patterns among civilly committed addicts, "Journal of American Medical Association," 208(12):2297–2301, 1969.

Lieberman, L., and Brill, L., Rational authority and the treatment of narcotics offenders, "Bulletin of Narcotics," 20:33–37, January–March 1968.

President's Commission on Law Enforcement and Administration of Justice, Task force report: narcotics and drug abuse annotations and consultants' papers (Washington, D.C.: U.S. Government Printing Office).

Vaillant, G. E., A 12-year follow-up of New York City addicts, I. The relation of treatment to outcome, "American Journal of Psychiatry," 122:727–737, 1966.

Vaillant, G. E., A 12-year follow-up of New York narcotic addicts, IV. Some determinants and characteristics of abstinence, "American Journal of Psychiatry," 123:573–584, 1966.

Willmer, H. A., *Social Psychiatry in Action: A Therapeutic Community* (Springfield, Illinois: Charles C Thomas, 1958).

Winick, C., Maturing out of narcotic addiction, "Bulletin on Narcotics," 14(1):1–7, 1962.

Wood, R. W., California rehabilitation center, in Department of Health, Education, and Welfare, *Rehabilitating the Narcotic Addict, Vocational Rehabilitation Administration* (Washington, D.C.: U.S. Government Printing Office), pp. 149–161.

Wood, R. W., Civil narcotics program: a five-year progress report, in Department of Health, Education, and Welfare, *Rehabilitating the Narcotic Addict, Vocational Rehabilitation Administration* (Washington, D.C.: U.S. Government Printing Office).

Chapter 4

Bassin, A., Daytop village: on the way up from the addiction . . . stopover or cure? "Psychology Today," December 1968.

Casriel, D., *So Fair a House: Story of Synanon* (New Jersey: Prentice Hall, 1963).

Hartmann, D., A Study of drug-taking adolescents, "Psychoanalytic Study of the Child," 24:384–431, 1969.

Nyswander, M. E., Drug addictions, in S. Arieti (ed.), *American Handbook of Psychiatry* (New York: Basic Books, 1959), 1:614–622.

Rado, S., Narcotic bondage: a general theory of the dependence on narcotic drugs, "American Journal of Psychiatry," 114:165–170, 1957.

Rado, S., Psychoanalysis of pharmacothymia (drug addiction), "Psychoanalytic Quarterly," 2(1):1–23, 1933.

Ramirez, E., Drug addiction is not physiologic, "Medical World News," 9(34):55–67, 1968.

Ramirez, E., Mental health program of the Commonwealth of Puerto Rico, in Department of Health, Education, and Welfare, *Rehabilitating the Narcotic Addict, Vocational Rehabilitation Administration* (Washington, D.C.: U.S. Government Printing Office), pp. 171–181.

Ramirez, E., A new program to combat drug addiction in New York City, "British Journal of Addiction," 63(1&2):89–101, 1968.

Shelley, J. A., and Bassin, A., Daytop lodge: a new treatment approach for drug addicts, "Corrective Psychiatry," 11(4):186–195, 1965.

Sutherland, E. H., and Cressey, D. R., *Principles of Criminology*, 6th edition (Philadelphia: Lippincott, 1960), pp. 74–80.

Volkmann, R., and Cressey, D. R., Differential association and the rehabilitation of drug addicts, "American Journal of Sociology," 69(2):129–142, September 1963.

Wikler, A., A psychodynamic study of a patient during experimental self-regulated readdiction to morphine, "Psychiatric Quarterly," 26(2):270–293, April 1952.

Wikler, A., and Rasor, R. W., The psychiatric aspects of drug addiction, "American Journal of Medicine," 14:566–570, 1953.

Chapter 5

Askevold, F., The occurrence of paranoid incidents and abstinence delirium in abusers of amphetamine, "Acta Psychiatrica Scandinavica," 34:145–164, 1959.

Berman, L. P., and Vogelsang, P., Removal rates for barbiturates using two types of periotoneal dialysis, "New England Journal of Medicine," 270(2):77–80, 1964.

Brandon, S., and Smith, D., Amphetamines in general practice, "Journal of the College of General Practitioners," 5:603–606, 1964.

Cole, J. O., The stimulant drugs (unpublished manuscript, 1966).

Committee on Alcoholism and Addiction, Dependence on amphetamines and other stimulant drugs, "Journal of American Medical Association," 197(12):1023–1027, 1967.

Connell, P. H., *Amphetamine Psychosis* (London: Chapman and Hall, 1958).

Connell, P. H., Clinical manifestations and the treatment of amphetamine types of dependence, "Journal of American Medical Association," 196:718, 1966.

Fischmann, V. S., Stimulant users in the California rehabilitation center, "International Journal of the Addictions" 3(1):113–130, 1968.

Fort, J., The problem of barbiturates in the U.S.A., "Bulletin of Narcotics," 16(1):17–35, 1964.

Isbell, H., Altschul, S., Kornetsky, C. H., Eisenman, A. J., Flanary, H. G., and Fraser, H. F., Chronic barbiturate intoxication, an experimental study, "Archives of Neurology and Psychiatry," 64:1–28, 1950.

Jaffe, J. H., The rapid development of physical dependence on barbiturates, "Journal of Pharmacological and Experimental Therapeutics," 150:130–145, 1969.

Kass, E., Retterstol, N., and Sirnes, T., Barbiturate intoxication and addiction as a public health program in Oslo, "WHO Bulletin on Narcotics," 11(3):15–28, 1959.

Kiloh, L. G., and Brandon, S., Habituation and addiction to amphetamines, "British Medical Journal," 5296:40–43, 1962.

Kornetsky, C. H., Psychological effects of chronic barbiturate intoxication, "Archives of Neurology and Psychiatry," 65:557–567, 1951.

Kraft, T., Successful treatment of a case of drinamyl addiction, "British Journal of Psychiatry," 114:1363–1364, 1968.

Kramer, J. C., Fischmann, V. S., and Littlefield, D. C., Amphetamine abuse: patterns and effects of high doses taken intravenously, "Journal of American Medical Association," 201:305–309, 1967.

Lemere, F., The danger of amphetamine dependency, "American Journal of Psychiatry," 123(5):569–572, 1966.

Rockwell, D., Amphetamine use and abuse in psychiatric patients (presented at meeting of American College of Neuropsychopharmacology, 1966).

Russo, J. R., *Amphetamine Abuse* (Springfield, Illinois: Charles C Thomas, 1968).

Smith, D., Speed freaks vs. acidheads, conflicts between drug subcultures, "Clinical Pediatrics," 8:185–188, 1969.

Smith, D., and Wesson, D. R., A new method for the treatment of barbiturate dependence, "Journal of American Medical Association," 213:294–295, 1970.

Smith, D. E., Characteristics of dependence in high dose methamphetamine abuse, "International Journal of Addictions," 4(3): 435–459, 1969.

Smith, D. E., Physical vs. psychological dependence and tolerance in high dose methamphetamine abuse, "Clinical Toxicology" 2(1): 99–103, March 1969.

Thompson, T., and Pickens, R., Stimulant self-administration by animals: some comparisons with opiate self-administration, "Federation Proceedings," 29:6–12, January–February 1970.

Watson, R., Hartmann, E., and Schildkraut, J., Amphetamine withdrawal (paper presented at Meeting of American Psychiatric Association, Washington, D.C., May 7, 1971).

Wikler, A., Diagnosis and treatment of drug dependence of the barbiturate type, "American Journal of Psychiatry," 125(6):758–765, 1968.

Young, D., and Scoville, W. B., Paranoid psychosis in narcolepsy and the possible danger of benzedrine treatment, "Medical Clinics of North America," 22:637–645, 1938.

Chapter 6

Auerbach, R., and Rugowski, J. A., Lysergic acid diethylamide: effect on embryos, "Science," 157:1325–1326, 1967.

Bender, L., and Sankar, D. V. S., Chromosome damage not found in leukocytes of children treated with LSD-25, "Science," 159:749, 1968.

Blum, R., et al., The Utopiates: the use and users of LSD (New York: Atherton, 1964).

Cohen, M. M., Marinello, M. J., and Bock, N., Chromosomal damage in human leukocytes induced by lysergic acid diethylamide, "Science," 155:1417–1419, 1967.

Cohen, S., Lysergic acid diethylamide: side effects and complications, "Journal of Nervous and Mental Disease," 130:30–40, 1960.

Cohen, S., and Ditman, K. S., Prolonged adverse reactions to lysergic acid diethylamide, "Archives of General Psychiatry," 8:475–480, 1963.

Ditman, K., Proceedings of Meeting on Adverse Reactions to Hallucinogenic Drugs, National Institute of Mental Health, 1967.

Eggert, D. C., and Shagass, C., Clinical prediction of insightful response to a single large dose of LSD, "Psychopharmacologia," 9: 340–346, 1966.

Fink, M., *et al.*, Prolonged adverse reactions to LSD in psychotic subjects, "Archives of General Psychiatry," 15:450–454, 1966.

Freedman, D. X., On the use and abuse of LSD, "Archives of General Psychiatry," 18:330–347, 1968.

Freedman, D. X., Perspectives on the use and abuse of psychedelic drugs, in D. H. Efron (ed.), *Ethnopharmacologic Search for Psychoactive Drugs* (Washington, D.C.: U.S. Department of Health, Education, and Welfare, 1967).

Frosch, W. A., Robbins, E. S., and Stern, M., Untoward reactions to lysergic acid diethylamide (LSD) resulting in hospitalization, "New England Journal of Medicine," 273:1235–1239, 1965.

Geber, W. F., Congenital malformations induced by mescaline, LSD, and bromolysergic acid in the hamster, "Science," 158:265–267, 1967.

Gioscia, V., LSD subcultures: acidoxy vs. orthodoxy (presented at Meeting of American Orthopsychiatric Association, Chicago, Illinois, March 1968).

Glass, G. S., and Bowers, M. B., Chronic psychosis associated with long-term psychotomimetic drug abuse, "Archives of General Psychiatry," 23:97–103, August 1970.

Holmstead, B., Historical survey, in D. H. Efron (ed.), *Ethnopharmacologic Search for Psychoactive Drugs* (Washington, D.C.: U.S. Department of Health, Education, and Welfare, 1967).

Irwin, S., and Egozcue, J., Chromosomal abnormalities in leukocytes from LSD-25 users, "Science," 157:313–315, 1967.

Jarvik, M., The behavioral effects of psychotogens, in R. C. DeBold and R. C. Leaf (eds.), *LSD, Man and Society* (Middletown, Conn.: Wesleyan, 1968).

Judd, L. L., Brandkamp, W., and McGlothlin, W. H., Comparison of the chromosome patterns obtained from groups of continued users, former users and non-users of LSD-25 (presented at the 124th Annual Meeting, American Psychiatric Association, Boston, Mass., 1968).

Katz, M. M., Waskow, I. E., and Olsson, J., Characterizing the psychological state produced by LSD, "Journal of Abnormal Psychology," 73:14, 1968.

Lettvin, J., You can't even step in the same river twice, "Natural History," 76(4):6–12, October 1967.

Linton, H. B., Langs, R. J., and Paul, I. H., Retrospective alterations of the LSD experience, "Journal of Nervous and Mental Disease," 138(5):409–423, 1964.

Louria, D. B., Statement, in *Increased Controls Over Hallucinogens and Other Dangerous Drugs: Hearings on H.R. 14096; H.R. 15355*, Subcommittee on Public Health and Welfare of the Committee on Interstate and Foreign Commerce, House of Representatives, 90th Cong., 2nd sess. (Washington, D.C.: U.S. Government Printing Office, 1968).

McGlothlin, W., Cohen, S., and McGlothlin, M., Long-lasting effects of LSD in normals, "Archives of General Psychiatry," 17:521–532, 1967.

McGlothlin, W., Cohen, S., and McGlothlin, M., Short-term effects of LSD on anxiety, attitudes and performance, "Journal of Nervous and Mental Disease," 139:266–273, 1964.

Meyer, R. E. (ed.), Adverse reactions to hallucinogenic drugs with background papers, Public Health Service Publication #1810 (Chevy Chase, Md.: National Clearing House, Mental Health Information, 1967).

Osmond, H., Proceedings of Meeting on Adverse Reactions to Hallucinogenic Drugs, National Institute of Mental Health, 1967.

Rosenthal, S., Persistent hallucinosis following repeated administration of hallucinogenic drugs, "American Journal of Psychiatry," 121:238–244, 1964.

Schick, J. F., Smith, D. E., and Meyers, F. H., Patterns of drug use in the Haight-Ashbury neighborhood, "Clinical Toxicology," 3(1): 19–56, March 1970.

Shagass, C., Proceedings of Meeting on Adverse Reactions to Hallucinogenic Drugs, National Institute of Mental Health, 1967.

Silverman, J., Proceedings of Meeting on Adverse Reactions to Hallucinogenic Drugs, National Institute of Mental Health, 1967.

Smith, D. E., Proceedings of Meeting on Adverse Reactions to Hallucinogenic Drugs, National Institute of Mental Health, 1967.

Smith, D. E., Use of LSD in the Haight-Ashbury, Observations of a neighborhood clinic, "California Medicine," 110(6):472–476, June 1969.

Smith, D. E., and Rose, A. J., Health problems in urban and rural "crash pad" communes, "Clinical Pediatrics," 9:534–537, 1970.

Soskin, W. F., and Korchin, S. J., Therapeutic explorations with adolescent drug users (presented at the American Orthopsychiatric Association Meeting, Chicago, Illinois, March 1968).

Ungerleider, J. T., Proceedings of Meeting on Adverse Reactions to

Hallucinogenic Drugs, National Institute of Mental Health, 1967.

Ungerleider, J. T., Fisher, D. D., Fuller, M., and Caldwell, A., The "bad trip"—the etiology of the adverse LSD reaction, "American Journal of Psychiatry," 124:1483–1490, 1968.

U.S., Congress, House, Committee on Interstate and Foreign Commerce, *Drug Abuse Control Amendments of 1965: Hearings on H.R. 2,* 89th Cong., 1st sess., January 27, 28, February 2, 9, and 10, 1965 (Washington, D.C.: U.S. Government Printing Office, 1965).

Warkany, J., Proceedings of Meeting on Adverse Reactions to Hallucinogenic Drugs, National Institute of Mental Health, 1967.

Willmer, H. A., Drugs, hippies and doctors, "Journal of American Medical Association," 206(6):1272–1275, November 4, 1968.

Zellweger, H., McDonald, J. S., and Abbo, G., Is lysergic acid diethylamide a teratogen? "Lancet," 1066–1068, November 18, 1967.

Chapter 7

Becker, H. S., History, culture and subjective experience, an exploration of the social basis of drug-induced experiences, "Journal of Health and Social Behavior," 8:163–176, 1967.

Clark, L., and Nakashima, E., Experimental studies of marihuana, "American Journal of Psychiatry," 125:379–384, 1968.

Clark, L. D., Hughes, R., and Nakashima, E., Behavioral effects of marihuana, "Archives of General Psychiatry," 23:193–198, 1970.

Hollister, L. E., Marihuana in man: three years later, "Science," 172:21–29, April 2, 1971.

Hollister, L. E., and Gillespie, H. K., Marihuana, ethanol, and dextroamphetamine, "Archives of General Psychiatry," 23:199–203, 1970.

Hollister, L. E., Richard, R. K., and Gillespie, B. A., Comparison of tetrahydrocannabinol and synhexyl in man, "Clinical Pharmacology and Therapeutics," 9:783–791, 1968.

Isbell, H., Gorodetzsky, C. W., Jasinski, D., Claussen, U., Spulak, F. V., and Korte, F., Effects of (-)-delta-9-trans-tetra-hydrocannabinol in man, "Psychopharmacologia," 11:184–188, 1967.

Jones, R. T., Report to American College of Neuropharmacology, conference on marihuana, December 1970.

Jones, R. T., and Stone, G. C., Psychological studies of marijuana in man (presented at the 125th Annual Meeting of the American Psychiatric Association Bal Harbour, Florida, May 1969).

Keeler, M. H., Motivation for marihuana use, a correlate of adverse reaction, "American Journal of Psychiatry," 125:386–390, 1968.

King, F. W., Marijuana and LSD usage among male college students: prevalence rate, frequency, and self-estimates of future use, "Psychiatry," 32:265–276, 1969.

Lemberger, L., Silberstein, S. D., Axelrod, J., and Kopin, I. J., Marihuana: studies on the disposition and metabolism of delta-9-tetrahydrocannabinol in man, "Science," 170:1320–1322, 1970.

Lemberger, L., Tamarkin, N. R., Axelrod, J., and Kopin, I. J., Delta-9-tetrahydrocannabinol: metabolism and disposition in long-term marihuana smokers, "Science," 173:72–74, 1971.

McMillan, D. E., Harris, L. S., Frankenheim, J. M., and Kennedy, J. S., 1-delta-9-trans-tetrahydrocannabinol in pigeons: tolerance to the behavioral effects, "Science," 169:501–503, 1970.

Manheimer, D. I., Mellinger, G. D., and Balter, M. B., Marijuana use among urban adults, "Science," 166:1544–1545, 1969.

Mechoulam, R., Marihuana chemistry, "Science," 168:1159–1166, 1970.

Melges, F. T., Tinklenberg, J. R., Hollister, L. E., and Gillespie, H. K., Temporal disintegration and depersonalization during marihuana intoxication, "Archives of General Psychiatry," 23:204–210, 1970.

Meyer, R. E., et al., Administration of marihuana to heavy and casual users, "American Journal of Psychiatry," August 1971, 128:198–204.

Mirin, S. M., Shapiro, L. M., Meyer, R. E., Pillard, R. C., and Fisher, S., Casual versus heavy use of marijuana: a redefinition of the marijuana problem, "American Journal of Psychiatry," 127:1134–1140, 1971.

Report to Congress, Secretary of Health, Education, and Welfare, Marihuana and health, January 31, 1971 (Washington, D.C.: U.S. Government Printing Office, 1971).

Waskow, I. E., Olsson, J. E., Salzman, C., and Katz, M. M., Psychological effects of tetrahydrocannabinol, "Archives of General Psychiatry," 22:97–107, 1970.

Weil, A. T., Adverse reactions to marihuana, "New England Journal of Medicine," 282:997–1000, 1970.

Weil, A. T., Zinberg, N. E., and Nelsen, J. M., Clinical and psychological effects of marihuana in man, "Science," 162:1234–1242, 1968.

Index

Department of Housing and Urban
Development (HUD): 2, 132,
135, 136, 146
Department of Justice: 5–6, 133,
135, 136, 146
Department of Labor: 136
Department of Transportation: 136
Detoxification: 21–23, 24, 25, 26,
30, 38, 77
Dextroamphetamine: 89
Diet pills: 15, 90
Diskind, M., and Klonsky, G.: 55
Dole, Dr. Vincent: xv, 38–39,
40, 41, 44
Dole-Nyswander program: 40,
41, 42–43
Dopamine: 96
Doriden. See Glutethimide
"Dropping out": 109, 110–112
Drug antagonists: 21
"Drug hunger": 39, 40, 53, 88
DuPont, R. L.: 139

Encounter groups. See Groups,
exhortative and confrontation
Equanil. See Meprobamate
Ethyl alcohol: 29
Euphoria: 40, 97, 116
Ex-addicts: in drug addiction
prevention programs, 13,
70–72, 79

FIRST: 69–70
Federal Bureau of Narcotics. See
Bureau of Narcotics and
Dangerous Drugs
Federal Bureau of Prisons: 2,
57, 130, 136
Federal Civil Commitment
Program: 36, 54, 56–57, 59
Federal Drug Administration
(FDA): 44–45, 78, 120
Fluphenazine enanthate: 94
Fort Worth Hospital: 1,
4, 21, 25, 57

Freedman, A. M., and Fink, M.:
49, 50, 51–52
Freedman, David: xv
Frosch, W. A.: 9, 99, 101

Gearing, Dr. Francis: 42,
43–44, 45
Geis: 58
Genetic risk: 96, 108
Germany: 8
Ghettos: 4, 7, 9–10
Gover, Edward: 61
Glutethimide (Doriden): 86
Goldstein, A.: 41
Great Britain: 5, 20
Group therapy. See Therapy, group
Groups, exhortative and
confrontation: 63–76

HEW. See Department of Health,
Education and Welfare
HUD. See Department of Housing
and Urban Redevelopment
Haight-Ashbury: 103–104, 107
Haight-Ashbury Medical Clinic:
104
Halfway houses: 26, 58
Hallucinogens: 9, 10, 11–12, 14,
27, 90, 92, 96–112
Harrison Narcotics Act: 4
Hashish. See Marihuana
Heroin: xiii, 5, 19–79, 90, 94, 150
Hippies: 8
Hollister, L. E.: 114, 116
Hypnotic-sedative drugs: 29,
83–95

Illinois Drug Addiction Program:
36, 76, 136, 138–139
Investigational New Drug
Application (I.N.D.): 45
Isbell, H., et al.: 116

Jaffe, Dr. Jerome H.: xiii, xiv, xv,

Pharmacological treatments. *See* Methadone; Narcotic-blocking drugs
"Pharmacothymic cycle": 91, 93
Phenobarbital: 88
Phenothiazines: 91, 92, 94, 95, 100, 105
Phoenix House: 69, 70, 72
Prevention programs: 10–15, 121–122
Promethazine: 24
Psychedelic drugs. *See* Hallucinogens
"Psychedelic experience": 97
Psychological treatments: 61–79
Psychosis: 91, 92
Public Health Service: 134
Puerto Rico: drug program, 72–73

Quinine: 21

Ramirez, Dr. E.: 65–66, 69, 72, 73, 138
Rasor, Dr. Robert: 57
Rehabilitation: at community level, 142–153; at Federal level, 130–137; of heroin addict, 19–79; at state level, 138–142
Relapsing behaviors, chronic: 19, 26–34
Resident treatment: 78
Rio Piedras project: 69
Riverside Hospital: 78
Robbins, L. N., and Murphy, G. E.: 9
Robinson vs. California: 54
Rockefeller, John D.: 54, 55, 56
Rockefeller University: 38
Rosenthal, S.: 99

Safe Streets Act: 2, 133, 135
Schizophrenia: 8, 91
Scopolamine: 105
Secobarbital: 85
Sedatives. *See* Hypnotic-sedative drugs

Serotonin: 96
Sleeping pills: 15
Smith, David: *xv*, 88, 90, 102
Solvent sniffing: *xiv*
Special Action Office on Drug Abuse Prevention: 45, 46, 128, 136–137
"Speed": 90, 91, 92, 93–94
Strychnine: 105
Succinyl choline: 75–76
Suicide: 20, 85
Sutherland: 66
Sweden: amphetamine epidemic in, 94
Synanon, 22, 32, 58, 64, 66, 68, 70, 71

Tetrahydrocannabinol (THC): 116, 120
Texas Christian University: 31
Thalidomide: 108
Therapy, group: 63–76
"Total body orgasm": 91
Tranquilizers: 24, 92

Ungerleider, J. T.: 99
U.S. Public Health Service: 78, 134

Vaillaint, G. E.: 55–56
Veterans Administration (VA): 2, 133, 136
Volkmann, R.: 66

Wieland, W. F.: 40, 41
Wikler, Abraham: 29, 39
Wilmer, Harry: 58
Winick, Charles: 56
Withdrawal syndrome: amphetamine, 91–92; barbiturate, 87–88; heroin, 19, 21–26, 29, 34
Wood, Roland: 57, 58

Yablonsky: 71
Yale Medical School: 69